Mediation
Transforming Conflict through Communication

Christina M. Sabee, PhD
San Francisco State University

Thom Massey, MA
Stanford University

Bea Herrick
*Santa Clara County's
Dispute Resolution Program Services*

KENDALL/HUNT PUBLISHING COMPANY
4050 Westmark Drive   Dubuque, Iowa 52002

Copyright © 2008 by Christina M. Sabee, Thom Massey, and Bea Herrick

ISBN 978-0-7575-5087-4

Kendall/Hunt Publishing Company has the exclusive rights to reproduce this work,
to prepare derivative works from this work, to publicly distribute this work,
to publicly perform this work and to publicly display this work.

Printed in the United States of America
10 9 8 7 6 5 4 3 2 1

Contents

About the Authors

Christina M. Sabee (PhD, Northwestern University) is Assistant Professor of Communication Studies at San Francisco State University. Dr. Sabee teaches and researches in the areas of mediation and conflict management and volunteers as a mediator in her community.

Thom Massey (MA, Stanford University) is Associate Dean of Students and Multicultural Educator at Stanford University. Mr. Massey directs the development of the student mediation program on his campus and conducts trainings in mediation and multicultural education and volunteers as a mediator in his community.

Bea Herrick is the training coordinator for the Santa Clara County Dispute Resolution Program Services. In addition to her work with all facets of the DRPS, she works with colleges and universities in the San Francisco Bay Area to train and educate students, faculty, and staff in mediation skills.

Acknowledgements

The authors would like to thank the members of the Campus Consortium, with whom we have enjoyed learning about, and developing programs around, mediation and conflict management in our communities.

1

Introduction

We come into conflict with people every day. As you will read in Chapter Two, one way we learn and grow as individuals and societies is through conflict. Most of the time, we might like to think that we can resolve our differences with others in an acceptable way. However, at times disputes among people are too complicated for them to handle on their own. There may be important legal issues to consider, or high emotional involvement from all people in the dispute. Sometimes, people find themselves at an impasse—unable to think of other ways to work through their differences.

Consider a couple who have decided to divorce. Divorcing couples often have strong emotions about ending their relationship. They may feel like they have tried to work through the problems in their relationship, but they have come to an impasse. They may also be concerned about their livelihoods after becoming divorced since they will no longer be sharing household expenses. If they have children, they may be concerned about custody of their children and visitation.

Many divorcing couples have difficulty coming to resolution about their concerns on their own. In some cases, each party hires a lawyer, discusses their interests with the lawyer, and then waits for the two lawyers to reach a settlement agreement acceptable to both parties. If they are unable to come to a settlement agreement, the lawyers may suggest that the two parties state their cases before a judge in court and have the judge make a decision for them.

ACTIVITY 1.1

Pair up with another individual in your class. Imagine that you are lawyers for a couple that has decided to divorce. The couple has been having difficulty agreeing on who should get what after the divorce. Below is a list of the things that are in dispute—each side has said that they want to have all of the following things. However, as lawyers, you want to find a resolution so the couple will not have to go to court. See if you and your partner can come up with a settlement plan to sell to the divorcing couple.

House—3 bedrooms, 2 bathrooms

Vacation House—3 bedrooms, 2 bathrooms, "up north"

Children—7 year old boy, 4 year old girl

Photo albums

Furniture (in both houses)

1. What settlement plan did you come up with?

    Mom gets main house + kids during week. Furniture stays in each house. Albums will be duplicated. Dad gets vacay house → its worth more. Kids on weekend

2. Why did you decide on the plan that you did? What was easy about the decision? What was difficult about the decision?

    _____

    _____

    _____

3. Do you wish that you could have had more information? If so, what?

    _____

    _____

    _____

4. Do you wish that the process might have been different? If so, how?

    _____

    _____

    _____

WHAT IS MEDIATION?

Mediation is only one of a number of different ways that people use to settle their disputes. In mediation, *disputing parties call upon the services of a neutral, independent party to help them come to a resolution on their own*. Mediation can be approached in many different ways; but no matter how a mediator approaches mediation, the following main characteristics define the process.

1. **Outside Party:** Mediation always brings an "outside" party into a dispute to help parties in conflict come to a resolution. The mediator is often called a "third party"; however, since not all disputes are between only two people, we like to use the term "outside party." This outside party should have no financial or personal interests in the dispute. While in select cases, parties may know the mediator before mediation begins; in most cases, the mediator is unknown to the parties before the mediation process.

2. **Neutral:** Mediators are not just "outside" parties. It is also important that mediators are *neutral* outside parties. Mediators need to examine their assumptions and beliefs before entering into a mediation session because they need to be prepared to help all parties equally. Mediators can neither take sides nor make recommendations. A mediator needs to be able to question the parties without attacking them, help the parties communicate their needs and interests, help the parties listen to each other in a productive and active manner, and build a strong level of trust with the parties in order for the process to work. A mediator who is not neutral, or who appears to take sides in a dispute, is not likely to earn the trust of all of the parties involved and is, therefore, unlikely to be successful.

3. **Decisions by the Parties:** Unlike in court, mediators do not make decisions or recommendations about resolutions for disputes. While they listen to the parties and help them identify what is important to them and hear what is important to the others, they do not make decisions. In mediation, the mediator helps the parties come up with resolutions on their own. The mediator will help the parties brainstorm and work through options (after they have agreed upon their needs and interests); however, if the parties do not come up with the ideas, they are not a part of the final resolution. As you will see more clearly in the next section, a judge or an arbitrator may suggest certain resolutions for disputing parties, but mediators do not.

4. **Focuses on Relationships:** Rather than focusing solely on the resolution of a dispute, mediation focuses on working through the relationships of the disputing parties. Because mediators help the parties communicate with each other and agree upon a resolution together, parties are often empowered to

communicate with each other more effectively following a mediation session. Mediation is often a recommended process for dispute resolution when parties are family members, colleagues at work, or neighbors, because these parties will often need to continue some sort of relationship after the resolution of their dispute. If a judge or other empowered person makes a decision that not all parties agree with, there may be resentment and the parties may not effectively communicate with each other afterwards. However, with mediation, the parties all agree upon the resolution and learn to work through differences more productively during the process.

5. **Confidential:** Mediations are confidential conversations that occur among the mediators and parties. Mediators do not discuss what occurs in a mediation session with anyone outside of the mediation itself. Also, the parties who are involved in the mediation may not discuss the details with anyone outside of the mediation unless everyone agrees. Mediators and parties will typically sign a confidentiality agreement at the beginning of mediation so that everyone is clear about confidentiality from the start.

WHAT MEDIATION IS NOT

Since there are a number of different ways for people to resolve their disputes, mediation can be confused with other forms of dispute resolution. In this section, we will consider a few of the alternatives disputing parties can use in seeking assistance with their disputes (for an in-depth discussion of alternative dispute resolution, see Goldberg, Sander & Rogers, 1999).

Litigation

Litigation is a well-known form of dispute resolution. When people participate in litigation, they formalize their dispute in a prescribed manner so that the civic legal system can assist them in their resolution. While litigation may take place in many different ways, the basic process involves submitting a complaint and empowering a judge to make a decision about the resolution of the complaint. If one party makes a decision to take another to court, once the process starts, it is not voluntary for the parties—they must complete what they started following specific legal rules (Goldberg, Sander & Rogers, 1999).

In some cases, individual parties will submit a complaint on their own and appear in court with the other party(ies) to state their cases. A judge will listen to each party and ask appropriate questions. Then, the judge will render an official decision about the resolution of the dispute. In some cases, the judge will decide that one party's case is stronger than the other in which case the stronger party's case would "win." For instance, in a dispute among roommates about who should pay for repairs from the security deposit, the judge may find that one party should pay the bulk of the deposit because that party caused the bulk of the need for repairs.

In other cases, disputing parties will seek the assistance of lawyers to help them maneuver the court system. Because the system is highly structured and has many specific rules, unless individuals have had legal training, they might find it difficult to go through litigation without the support of an expert in the area. In these cases, individual parties will discuss their interests with a lawyer who holds their discussions confidential. Then, the lawyer will strategically communicate through the legal system to help the client appear to have the strongest case. Either lawyers can argue for their clients in front of a judge, or they can work with each other to come up with a settlement option that they bring to their clients for agreement.

In litigation, while parties are consulted through questioning and representation about their interests and needs by their lawyers, they are ultimately asking an outside party (either their lawyers or a judge) to come up with the appropriate resolution for their dispute. Once one party starts this process, it cannot end except through specific legal means. In mediation, however, parties are expected to *voluntarily* work together to come up with a resolution agreeable to all. Even though lawyers and judges can and do serve as mediators for disputes, their roles in mediations are much different from when they act as lawyers and judges. Probably, the greatest difference is that of *who* is empowered to create and decide upon an acceptable resolution.

Litigation is not always an ideal form of dispute resolution because it usually takes a long time (months or years); it is expensive to pay lawyers and court costs; and once the process starts, it is no longer in the hands of the disputing parties. For those with disputes that are not appropriate for the court, other options exist.

Arbitration

Arbitration is another form of dispute resolution, which, like litigation, empowers an outside party to make a decision about an appropriate resolution based on information supplied by the disputing parties. Typically, disputing parties agree on the selection of a neutral, outside party to act as an arbitrator. They will also agree on some objective standards that the arbitrator will use to make a decision. After the parties agree upon the arbitrator and the arbitration criteria (rules), the arbitrator meets with the parties to obtain relevant information and then makes a decision about how to resolve the dispute. This decision is typically binding in that the parties must follow it whether or not they agree (Goldberg, Sander & Rogers, 1999).

Arbitration has some advantages in that parties can select an expert in their conflict area as an arbitrator, it is quicker and costs less than litigation, and once a decision is reached, the dispute is effectively over. This is both desired and appropriate for some disputes. However, for some disputes, the lack of focus on a continuing relationship, the lack of control by the parties, and the finality of the decision-making can all seem wrong. Mediation offers an opportunity for parties to be more involved in the outcome of their dispute than arbitration.

Counseling

Outside of the legal system, parties in conflict often seek the assistance of counselors. This is particularly appropriate for family and romantic relationships. Counselors can help disputing parties work out their problems through directed questioning and communication exercises.

Like mediation, counseling usually focuses on the relationships of the parties involved. It also will focus on the feelings and psychological needs of the parties. Unlike mediation, counseling is not typically a method of conflict *resolution*. That is, people will be encouraged to talk through their issues and feelings, but counselors will not usually work toward helping parties brainstorm a solution.

Counselors are also not necessarily neutral. For example, a counselor may focus on the needs of one person who seems to need the most help at that particular time. Counselors are more concerned with the psychological health of their clients than with the needs of all disputing parties or the resolution of a conflict.

Beginning mediators often struggle to understand the specific roles of a mediator in contrast to the roles discussed above. Mediators should reach a gentle balance between focusing on the needs and feelings of disputing parties without *counseling* them. Another gentle balance must be reached between helping parties come up with the best possible solutions for their dispute without giving them *recommendations* and making *decisions* for them. It is also important to work through the difference between asking questions to find out the "facts" (as a litigator or arbitrator would) and asking questions to highlight *interests* and *needs* (as a mediator would). Throughout this text, exercises and activities will help you specifically to work through the skills required in effective mediation without crossing over into other methods of dispute resolution.

THE MEDIATION PROCESS

The mediation process is both fluid and flexible. As we describe the process below, please keep in mind that the purpose of mediation is to help the parties come up with a resolution that works for them. In some cases, mediators find themselves repeating steps in the process, skipping steps in the process, or moving back and forth between steps several times before moving on. Here, we give you a general overview of the mediation process, so that you can follow along as we practice aspects of mediation throughout the course.

Case Development

The mediation process starts with what we call "case development." Usually, one of the disputing parties will contact a mediator, or a mediation service, to ask for assistance in resolving a conflict. In other cases, one or all of the conflicting parties may be *referred* to a mediator or mediation service. In any case, the "case development" starts when a mediator is introduced to at least one of the parties. Then, it is that mediator's job to find out important background information such as who the disputing parties are, their contact information, their availability for attending a mediation session, and some basic understanding of the story behind the conflict. While it seems like anyone might be able to collect this information, it is actually important that a person trained in communication skills, such as those used in mediation, conduct the case development. Parties often have difficulty communicating about disputes even when they are talking about them to a neutral party. Case developers should maintain a neutral stance while helping the parties work through their stories during this first phase. Case developers also should be sensitive to the needs of all parties because they will be setting up an initial meeting with the conflicting parties, acting either as the mediator, or by selecting another trained mediator to work with the parties.

Introduction

Once the mediation is set up—usually this is a face-to-face meeting with the parties and the mediators—parties and mediators will come together. The mediator(s) will introduce themselves to the parties and have the parties introduce themselves to the mediator(s). During this stage, there is usually little talk about the actual dispute. Instead, the mediator will set the stage for what will happen during the process. They will explain the process to the parties and talk about the ground rules that everyone will follow during their meetings. As parties and mediators discuss, and become familiar with, the process they will be following, mediators will be modeling the communication behavior that they expect from everyone involved. During this stage, parties and mediators will also make a confidentiality agreement and be assured that everyone is present voluntarily. Mediation should never be forced.

Sharing Perspectives

After the mediation introduction process is finished, mediators will encourage the parties to share their perspectives. Parties will be encouraged to take turns talking about their interests in the dispute and their needs for a resolution. (The following chapters specifically deal with how perspectives can be most effectively shared during this opening stage of mediation.) At this point, it is important to recognize that the mediators will use important communication skills such as active listening, questioning, reframing, and coaching to help parties through this part of the mediation. When parties are able to share perspectives in a neutral environment, using conscientious and direct communication with each other, they set the stage for effective resolution of their conflict and for the future of their relationships.

Brainstorming

Once parties feel that they have fully discussed their needs and interest and the mediators recognize the parties' readiness to proceed, the process will move toward brainstorming. During this stage, the mediators will lead parties toward generating as many creative ideas that they can come up with to resolve their dispute. During this stage, no idea is too crazy. Parties should really stretch their imaginations and list as many things as they can to help facilitate the resolution process. While it is sometimes difficult to hold back, mediators should never participate in the actual brainstorming. Rather, they will usually take notes about ideas (often on a white board or easel so everyone can see) and continue to encourage parties to come up with ideas until everything is "on the table."

Problem Solving

After a successful brainstorming session, parties are ready to begin problem solving. Mediators will help them discuss which of the ideas they think would be most appropriate for their situation, and which ideas help to meet the needs of everyone involved. During this stage, mediators most often take the role of "reality checkers." As parties begin to agree about different ideas that will help them resolve their dispute, the mediators will continue to question them to make sure that all of the originally outlined needs are met by the solutions offered. When all parties believe that they have come up with a workable solution, the mediators will help them draft an agreement. Then all parties will sign the agreement and, hopefully, leave the mediation process with a better understanding of their relationship, themselves, and their future ability to resolve disputes.

In many cases, the mediation process is truly educational for the parties involved. As they learn to communicate their interests and concerns, as they learn to listen to each other, and as they learn that they actually *can* make progress toward a resolution with the other parties, each participant in the mediation leaves with a better understanding of themselves and others. While we might hope that people who participate in mediation would return to mediation in the future for assistance with resolving their disputes, we often find that people who have gone through mediation do not *need* to return in the future—because they have learned to resolve conflicts on their own.

OVERVIEW OF THE TEXT

In the following chapters, we will work through many different aspects of mediation—all with the goal of learning how to be effective mediators. We will first explore the nature of conflict and different ways of understanding how conflict affects our communications and us. We will then look into the different stages of the mediation process, work toward understanding the theories behind why mediators communicate the way that they do, and practice the communication skills that mediators need to help parties work through disputes. Finally, we will discuss the value of mediation in several specific cases we have dealt with during our own mediation careers. We will look into how mediation helped in those cases and what might have happened had the parties not participated in mediation to resolve their disputes.

2

Conflict and Communication

Writers of fiction, whether for books, screenplays, or short stories, follow a certain pattern in their writing that we all expect. There is usually a protagonist (lead character/hero) who runs into an obstacle (conflict) and finds some resolution at the end (good or bad). In fact, if you think about all of the books, stories, movies, television shows, etc. that you have enjoyed throughout the years, you will find some kind of "conflict" in each of them. They simply would not be interesting without it. Imagine if Spiderman spent the whole movie swinging around buildings and crawling up walls; or imagine that Ebenezer Scrooge fell into a deep sleep on the night before Christmas with no dreams of ghosts or past and future. What would the Peanuts comic strip be without Lucy pulling the football away from Charlie Brown at the very last moment? Or, perhaps Tony Soprano could just drop out of organized crime and lead a quiet life in suburbia!

Frankly, these stories would not be interesting without conflict. We *enjoy* conflict in our entertainment. Perhaps that is why reality television contests like *American Idol* are so popular—we want to see people overcome obstacles; we want to learn from mistakes; and we want to step out of our comfort zones (or at least we want to see others do it). When fiction writers call these obstacles *conflicts*, they refer to these kinds of opportunities wherein people *challenge* themselves and *grow*.

Conflict is a word with which we are all familiar. However, we often think about the conflicts that we observe in our entertainment as somehow different from the ones in which we engage interpersonally. While we may relish experiencing a conflict through a fictional account, we may also shy away from, and try to avoid, a conflict with a friend or a loved one. So why is it that we are more likely to see the growth and opportunity that conflict allows in fictional tales than we are in our own lives?

Before going further with our discussion about conflict and communication in this chapter, we would like you to consider the following two questions. Please feel free to take notes on these questions in the text box provided below.

---

1. How does conflict feel? _____

_____

_____

_____

2. Complete the following sentence: Conflict is like _____

_____

_____

_____

As you think about these questions, closely consider your answers. When you look at the words that you use to describe what conflict feels like, are they mostly negative? Are they mostly positive? Do they mirror other kinds of activities in which you engage? Can you think of other activities that make you feel the same way?

We have compiled some of the responses that past students have used to describe conflict. Look at some of those feelings (in Figure 2.1) and see how they compare to the ones you identified for yourself.

Figure 2.1: Feelings Associated with Conflict

Annoyance	Discouraged	Jealousy
Aggression/aggressive	Exhausted	Loss
Anger/angry	Envy	Lost
Arrogance	Fear	Misunderstanding
Apathy	Frustration	Oppression
Betrayal	Fragile	Power
Complacency	Guilt	Resent
Confusion	Helplessness	Self-righteousness
Competition	Hurt	Self-consciousness
Disrespect	Injustice	Used
Disenfranchised	Irritation	Vindictive

CASE STUDY

To Confront or Not to Confront

As you read the following case study, think about how Antonio and Lim are *feeling*. How does that affect their communication in this situation?

Antonio and his friend, Lim, were getting ready to go on a big camping trip together. They had gone on small trips in the past, but they had been planning a two-week camping trip during which they would hike to a remote area in the Sierra Mountains. They were both excited about the trip. Antonio had been doing some research about the camping trip and discovered that he and Lim needed to acquire some additional camping gear. The gear was expensive, but Antonio was working hard to either find used gear to buy or borrow gear from people he knew.

Antonio had found just about everything he needed and was able to keep within his budget. Also, he was able to borrow a couple of things for Lim. He and Lim met about a week before their trip to make sure that they had everything they needed. When Antonio showed Lim the items he had borrowed for him, Lim seemed quite pleased and thanked him. Lim had to find a couple more things for himself for the trip, but he was confident he would be able to get them in time.

When they got together to leave for the trip, Antonio noticed that Lim was not bringing the items that he had borrowed for him. When he asked Lim about it, Lim shared that he had already acquired those items, so he used the ones that Antonio gave him to trade for items that he did not already have. Antonio was upset because he was supposed to return those items to their owners after the trip. However, it was clear that Lim had not realized Antonio had borrowed the items—it seemed that Lim thought Antonio owned the items and was giving them to him.

Now Antonio faced a choice. He was really upset and angry about the situation. He was also nervous about how he would explain what had happened to the people from whom he borrowed the items. However, he was about to leave on this two-week trip with his friend and he did not think Lim meant to put him in that position. He was also concerned that bringing up the matter now might put a bad spin on the trip. He was not sure if he should tell Lim what happened. He did not want to ruin the trip by making Lim feel bad, but he also did not want to hold in his feelings and resent Lim for the entire trip.

1. What should Antonio do in this situation?

   _____

   _____

   _____

2. What kinds of feeling words do you think would describe how Antonio feels?

   _____

   _____

   _____

3. What are Antonio's main concerns about confronting Lim? What are his main concerns about not confronting Lim?

   _____

   _____

   _____

In any situation in which two or more people find themselves in conflict, the decision about whether to address the conflict becomes very important. Some people will feel that the issue is not important enough to warrant the discomfort of a conflict. Others might feel that addressing the conflict is the only way for them to move forward. Still others will make different decisions—and those decisions will always be dependent on both the *context of the situation* and the person's *approach to conflict*.

SOCIAL CONSTRUCTIONISM

Many textbooks and research papers about conflict include a definition of conflict at their outset. However, we would like to introduce you to a *way of thinking* before we introduce you to a definition. Please consider the following two circumstances as we begin.

Case #1

Sydney, a department manager, works at a big corporate office where there seems to be a lot of bureaucracy to wade through whenever a decision needs to be made. She has been quite frustrated with the process. Whenever she comes up with a way that she believes will help the company operate more efficiently, the idea needs to go through so many channels and offices that it is inevitably implemented in an entirely different way than she originally imagined, and she rarely retains credit for her ideas.

Recently, she came up with an idea that she thought would help the company produce their product in a much more efficient way. She ran the numbers and found that if she implemented the strategy immediately in her own department that she would be able to save enough money to hire three more desperately needed workers. However, when she sent the idea to her superior for approval, she found herself waiting for six weeks while valuable resources were being wasted. There was just so much red tape!

Finally, she heard back from her superior; however, instead of approval, her superior told her that one of the vice presidents would like her to be a part of a task force that would implement an efficiency plan across the company. Sydney was devastated—first, she would not be able to implement her plan until after the task force had approved it; and second, she did not get to lead the task force! She would just be one of seven other people working on messing up an idea that she had come up with.

Sydney felt terrible and spent the next week looking for other employment. After she applied for several other jobs, she was offered a position at another company and gave her notice to her current employer.

1. What kind of environment did Sydney find herself in at work?

   _____

   _____

   _____

2. Was Sydney in a conflict? If so, how would you describe it? Who was it with?

   _____

   _____

   _____

3. What three words do you believe best describe Sydney's feelings in this situation?

   _____

   _____

   _____

Case #2

Leslie was a leader for her department at the company where she worked. She enjoyed her career at this company, in part because of the way that they included their employees in important decisions. The founder of the company had been frustrated with other companies because high-level management was making decisions with no input from other employees. Thus, when she started the company, she made sure that there were opportunities for all company employees to have their voices heard. She also instituted a policy that top-level management would never make decisions without first consulting employees throughout the company.

Even though Leslie was the leader of only a single department, her appreciation for the way employee voice was valued at her company meant that she thought critically about the entire company—not just her own department. Since demand for the product they produced was high, and Leslie knew she could use two or three new workers in her department, she brought together a group of her employees to brainstorm ways that they might make it possible, given their limited funds, to hire more employees. They came up with a few ideas and sent them on to Leslie's superiors who were pleased to consider them.

Leslie's initiative paid off. Many other people in the company saw the ideas that her department had put together and really liked them. Several people from around the company worked with Leslie to come up with an overall plan to implement these cost-saving measures throughout the company, which resulted in a substantial savings. Not only was Leslie able to hire more workers, but other departments were able to do so as well. Leslie's initiative in coordinating the initial proposal and her work in putting the final plan together also resulted in her promotion.

1. What kind of environment did Leslie find herself in at work?

    _____

    _____

    _____

2. Was Leslie in a conflict? If so, how would you describe it? Who was it with?

    _____

    _____

    _____

3. What three words do you believe best describe Leslie's feelings in this situation?

_____

_____

_____

Would it surprise you to learn that these two scenarios involve the same company? Sydney and Leslie have almost identical positions at this company and find themselves working toward common goals. Yet, they have had entirely different experiences. In fact, if you look at the words that you have used to describe the feelings that each were having in these scenarios, you will probably find them drastically different. How could two people have such different experiences?

The way that we communicate can significantly shape our reality. Scholars of social constructionism have noted that we construct our basic understandings of the world through our interactions with other individuals; with institutions such as governments, religious organizations, and schools; and with the media that we enjoy (e.g., Pearce 1994). Our individual understandings of the world are created, in large part, by the kinds of interactions and experiences we have. Thus, a person who has been born into a family of privilege, has had accepting and loving relationships, and has been fortunate with opportunities for starting a career might see the world as a place ripe with opportunity for anyone who wants it. Another person, who was not born into such privilege and has not had as much good fortune with career and relationships, may see the world as a place that is unforgiving—a "dog-eat-dog" world. Our backgrounds, cultures, personalities, and social circles influence the way we approach the world and our experiences in it.

The way that we talk about conflict—the words we use to describe it, and the words we use to engage it—can shape how we feel about it. Moreover, these feelings about conflict can shape the ways that we engage in conflict. Take some time to think about your own background, culture, and social circles. How do you think they might influence the way you approach conflict? Do you approach conflict differently with some people than others? How might your social world contribute to the different ways that you approach conflict with different people?

STYLES OF CONFLICT

In addition to the different ways that people might frame conflict, many people also behave differently when they engage in conflict. Have you ever noticed that having conflicts with one person may be easier for you than having conflicts with another? Do some of your family and friends engage in conflict more often than others? Some of this may be due to their different conflict styles. While individuals may have many different types of styles, and various trainers and teachers of mediation may talk about the styles in different ways, we are going to introduce five conflict styles that individuals might use to approach conflict (Kilmann & Thomas, 1975).

Because the construction of our social world is shaped through interaction, we introduce these "styles" as *approaches to conflict*. However, the styles we initially seem to engage when in a conflict are influenced both by past experiences with conflict and by current interactions. Remember, as you read this section, that conflict "styles" are simply ways of describing approaches, and those approaches can change throughout interactions. Each conflict style we introduce is associated with the level of concern we initially have for our own interests and the level of concern we initially have for the other person's interests. Table 2.1 illustrates the different levels of interest as they compare to each other.

Sometimes individuals may feel that their interests in a conflict are not that important. Perhaps you do not really want to do the dishes again since you did them last night, and you would prefer that your roommate did them, but it does not bother you that much. In this instance, we would describe your concern for your own interests as low. When concerns for our own interests are low, we typically behave in one of two ways when we approach conflict. First, we might avoid the conflict altogether. On the other hand, the conflict might not be important enough for us to engage the other person about our interests. In this case, you might just do the dishes without mentioning anything to the other person.

However, when we avoid conflicts, we are not just acting on concerns for our own interests; we are also acting on concerns for the other person's interests. Typically, when we avoid communicating about conflicts, we not only have low concern for our own interests, but also low concern for the other's interests. It might seem strange that avoiding a conflict about doing the dishes, when it really does not matter, is having a low concern for the other's interests. However, you are actually having high concern since you are doing the dishes for that person. Avoiding a conflict essentially means that you have stifled an opportunity for the other person to respond to your thoughts. So, let us say that you see the dishes in the sink and you see your roommate watching television in the other room. Even though it is your roommate's turn to do the dishes (which you both usually try to do right after dinner), you choose to avoid communicating about the conflict, and simply do the dishes yourself. In your mind, you might believe that your roommate now "owes you one" for the next night; or you might expect your roommate to do the dishes on the next night since you did them tonight. However, you did not discuss this with your roommate—you just did it.

This example of avoiding conflict may be no big deal; however, what if your roommate wanted to watch a particular news program before doing the dishes, and planned on doing them as soon as the news program was finished? Your roommate might feel badly upon realizing later that you already did the dishes. Or, perhaps your roommate was really counting on NOT doing the dishes the next night because of important evening plans. When your roommate goes to do the dishes after the television program and realizes that you have done the dishes, the roommate may feel obligated to do the dishes the next night, despite plans for not having to do that chore. The fact is, you showed low concern for your roommate's interests by avoiding the conflict. It seemed more important to you to avoid communicating than to address what might be your roommate;s legitimate concerns or issues.

So does this mean that if you do not really care *and* you want to respect your roommate's concerns that you need to have a shouting match about the dishes? Of course not. However, you can accommodate your roommate and communicate about the conflict at the same time. Simply saying something like "Hey, I know it's not my turn, but there are dishes in the sink that I'm going to do," gives your roommate an opportunity to respond and say, "Thanks, I appreciate that," or, "If you don't mind waiting, I will get to them right after this program."

Of course, we also have times when our concerns for our own interests are high. Doing the dishes may not be a big deal, but perhaps being fair about our financial responsibilities in the household is a big deal. If your roommate has neglected to pay their share of the rent, you may find yourself having a high concern for your interests. You may not be able to afford to pay for your roommate's share of the rent, or you may just not want to pay for your roommate's share because you are saving up for something else that is important to you. Sometimes, when we find that we have a high concern for our own interests, we will use a competing style of conflict. You may demand the rent from your roommate, "You're late with the rent—I need your share today." You may give your roommate an ultimatum, "You've not paid your rent in two months—you either need to pay by the end of the week, or you'll need to move out so I can find a new roommate." You may appeal to your roommate's sense of ethics, "You know it is not fair for me to have to pay your share of the rent—please give me your share by the end of the week." In any of these cases, you are making a demand. You frame your discussion with your roommate in such a way that by the end of the discussion you will either "win" by getting your roommate to pay the rent or "lose" if your roommate refuses to comply with your request. It also sets up a communication pattern that encourages your roommate to respond in either a submissive or a defensive manner. The roommate will either submit, "You're right, I will get you the money right away," or defend, "You know I'm strapped for cash since I lost my job—I couldn't possibly come up with the money right now!" Specific demands of this nature will not allow your roommate a lot of room for negotiation.

Competing is not the only way to approach a conflict in which we have high concern for our own interests. Collaborating is another way to work through conflicts. When we collaborate, we show high concern for our own interests as well as for those of the person with whom we are in conflict. In this case, if your roommate was late with the rent, you might approach the conflict as more of a collective problem to solve than as an added responsibility for yourself. Instead of making demands on your roommate, you might try to find out the causes for the problem, and how you and your roommate can work together to solve the problem. Depending on what you find out from your roommate, you may end up coming up with a payment plan, exchanging some financial responsibilities for others, or coming up with some other solution to your *collective* problem. When we approach conflict collaboratively, we are really recognizing that we are interdependent (i.e., dependent on each other) and that without working together, we will most likely not come up with an acceptable solution.

However, collaboration is hard work, and sometimes our concerns for our own and the other's interest are medium-high—but not really that high. Perhaps you have some concerns about the overall division of labor for chores around the house. You would like a fair resolution to the conflict, but you are not particularly concerned with what the resolution is. You also have some concerns that your roommate will think the resolution is fair. In this case, you may choose to compromise. You treat the problem as a resource problem with limited resources to be fairly divided. In this case, you would like to divide a certain number of chores equally between you and your roommate. This is different from collaboration because you are not treating this as an interdependent problem for which you need to come up with collective and creative solutions. Rather, you treat the issue as a resource issue and "divide up the pie."

Table 2.1: Conflict Styles and Interpersonal Concern

	Avoiding	Accommodating	Compromising	Competing	Collaborating
Concern for Self	Low	Low	Middle	High	High
Concern for Other	Low	High	Middle	Low	High

Adapted from Kilmann and Thomas (1975)

The styles used in conflicts are dependent upon a number of things. You may find that you use one or more of these styles more often than others. Maybe you find yourself avoiding conflict with a particular family member, or always competing in conflict with one of your colleagues. Everyone's approach to conflict, and the style they seem to use, will be influenced by their social worlds and experiences. Depending upon the situation, one style is sometimes more appropriate than another.

Most often, when people come to mediation, they seem to have high concerns for their own interests. They really want to work to find a solution that is acceptable for them. Mediation focuses on helping parties to use a collaborative style of conflict management. Thus, whether or not parties show up with a high concern for the other party's interests, mediators try to foster that concern so that both parties come to realize their interdependence with each other.

WHAT IS CONFLICT? AND WHY IS IT SO EMOTIONAL?

While each of us has an individual construction of what conflict is to us, one way that we like to define conflict for the purposes of mediation training is that "conflict is an expressed struggle between at least two parties who perceive incompatible goals, scarce resources, and interference from others in achieving their goals" (Wilmot & Hocker, 2000). You may have had experiences, which you thought of as conflict, but they do not really fit this definition. For example, many students say that they have "internal conflicts," in which the struggle is within themselves and not expressed or with another party. However, we have chosen to use this definition because it is appropriate for mediation practice.

The definition seems reasonable, yet conflict often does not seem reasonable. Many people, when asked to think about a recent conflict, will think of a situation that was uncomfortable, upsetting, and emotional. Conflict and emotion seem to go hand in hand, no matter how we end up expressing such emotion. Consider the following conversation:

Julia: *Hey Susan, I feel like even though we live together, I hardly ever see you anymore!*

Susan: *I know—we've all just been so busy lately.*

Julia: *Well, I guess, but I don't really feel that busy. I was really hoping we could spend some time together this weekend. Maybe go out shopping or something? Like we used to . . .*

Susan: *Oh, sounds like fun, but I'm totally booked! Friday and Saturday night I'm out with Marcus, and Saturday afternoon I'm supposed to meet his family for*

> *some birthday party or something. Then on Sunday, I'll have to catch up on my homework.*

Julia: *Oh, it just seems like you're always out with Marcus now. I mean, I'm really happy for you finding a boyfriend and everything, but it feels like you've kind of been neglecting your friends. Even Bianca and Hiromi have said the same to me.*

Susan: *Oh great. Now that I'm in a relationship that I'm happy with, you all find a way to try to ruin it. Relationships take a lot of work—I really love Marcus and it's important for me to spend time with him. If you were really my friends, you would understand that!*

Julia: *That's unfair! We are your friends—that's why we want to spend time with you. Friendships take work too, you know!*

While people may have a number of feelings in any given conflict, four particular feelings seem to pop up repeatedly. Communication scholars have found that anger, jealousy, hurt, and guilt are common emotions in conflicts and they affect the ways that people behave in conflicts. As you read the following section, think about how Susan and Julia are feeling during their conflict. When, if ever, do they feel these emotions?

Anger

Anger is an emotion often identified with conflict, and people feel it relatively often. Eighty percent of participants in a recent study reported a time that they had felt anger in the previous week (Carpenter & Halberstadt, 1996). Angry individuals suffer physiological symptoms as well, including raised heart rates, tense muscles, rapid breathing, and feeling of heat or flush (Scherer & Wallbott, 1994). Anger can potentially push a conflict down a destructive path unless it is not managed effectively. John Gottman, an expert in the field of relational communication, has conducted substantial research into the ways that emotion affects our communication. He has noted that strong physiological reactions to anger may make it difficult for an individual to stay calm and rational. Resulting behaviors might include repeating facial expressions that signify anger, contempt, disgust, or even communicating such emotions through harsh words (e.g., Gottman, 2001).

People who have difficulty controlling their anger in a conflict are seldom effective in resolving their disputes, and may end up damaging the relationship. Because the specific action associated with anger is to *attack* (Lazarus, 1991), angry people may become more aggressive. The rush of adrenaline a person feels when angry, and their attacking of the other person, may make them feel stronger and literally fuel the fire, resulting in verbal or physical attacks, or other behaviors such as slamming doors, stomping feet, etc. (Shaver et al., 1987). However, anger does not have to be handled destructively; those who understand how to handle their angry emotions constructively will use more *assertive* behaviors rather than *aggressive* behaviors (see Figure 2.2 for a comparison).

Anger is often triggered by some interruption of a person's goals, as suggested in the definition of conflict. However, there are seven specific events, or feelings, that might provoke anger in any given conflict (Canary et al., 1998). Likely reasons why people might become angry include:

- when their *identity*, or public face, is threatened;
- when they feel someone else is being *aggressive*;
- when they find themselves in a *frustrating* situation;
- when they perceive *unfairness or inequity*;
- when they believe someone (including themselves) has acted *incompetently*;
- when they believe their *relationship is threatened*;
- or, finally, people may have a *predisposition* toward being angry because of their personality or possibly from substance abuse of some sort.

Recalling Susan and Julia, do you think that either of them might have experienced anger in their conflict? If so, when?

Figure 2.2 Comparison of Passive, Aggressive, and Assertive Communication

	Passive Communication	Aggressive Communication	Assertive Communication
Directness of Communication	Indirect	Direct or Indirect	Direct
Who Is Respected?	Other only	Self only	Both self and other
Who Is Entitled?	Other	Self	Both self and other
Level of Concern for Self	Low	High	High
Level of Concern for Other	High	Low	High

Adapted from C. Parise (2004)

Jealousy

Jealousy is another common emotion associated with conflict. While we often think of jealousy as an emotion associated with romantic relationships, jealousy extends far beyond those relationships where conflict is concerned to professional relationships, sibling relationships, or even neighborhood disputes. Jealousy can be defined as "a unique emotion that is based on the perception that one's primary relationship is threatened by a third party" (Guerrero & Valley, 2006).

Jealousy seems to occur most often in romantic relationships. Insecurities that individuals feel about their relationship give rise to feelings of fear that they may "lose" a loved one, or anger at someone for trying to "steal" a loved one away. However, individuals may have these feelings and insecurities with many other types of relationships. One sibling may fear that his relationship with their parents is threatened when another sibling seems to be spending much more time with their parents. Or, an employee might feel jealousy over a co-worker's relationship with their superior. Certainly, friends may feel insecure about their relationships, as well. For instance, how do you think Susan or Julia feel jealousy in their conflict?

Another common emotion that we find ourselves working with in mediation cases is that of hurt. People feel *hurt* when they think that someone has injured them psychologically. Because this emotion is inherently interpersonal, in that it can only be experienced through interaction with another person, we find that it is common in situations when people feel they cannot manage a conflict by themselves. Many people who seek mediation do so about conflicts in which another person has hurt them.

A number of different kinds of situations can cause hurt. In general, though, people feel hurt when they believe that someone else questions or attacks their sense of self or their relationships. When others make accusations or threats, it is easy to see where another person might be hurt. Accusations have the specific intent of showing someone else's faults, and threats have the specific intent of punishing another person for some action (or inaction) (Vangelisti, 1994). When considering how these types of messages hurt people, it is also important to consider the assumptions that others make when they accuse and threaten. If people accuse you of being unreliable, they make the assumption that you have a trait of unreliability—that it is part of your identity—and in so doing they are attacking your sense of self.

Even messages that do not seem negative on their face can be hurtful. For instance, someone might be hurt by an evaluation received from someone else. Whether that evaluation is from a supervisor at work, a teacher, or a friend who is trying to help by evaluating the person's behavior (e.g., I think you are drinking too much), evaluations are related strongly to the identity of the person being evaluated and can be hurtful even if they are also helpful. Another person may tell a joke, which is not meant to be negative; but if it strikes a chord in someone's identity, that person may become hurt by it.

In our experience, it is important to uncover an individual's strong feelings in order for conflict to be manageable. While individuals may experience many other types of feelings during conflict, the three that we discussed are some of the most common. Please refer to the box of "feeling words" in this chapter to get an idea of how many different types of feelings people might have when they are in conflict.

In the next section, we begin to describe how mediators use communication to help people in conflict uncover those feelings and move forward toward resolution.

Figure 2.3: The "Lizard Brain"

Some people work to understand our emotional reactions as either conscious or unconscious events. Reactions that are conscious events are sometimes filtered through a part of our brain called the neo-cortex, which is a uniquely *human* and *rational* part of our brain.

Other events, however, may be filtered through an "older" part of our brain, which we share with other animals. This part of our brain, primarily concerned with our *survival*, is commonly called the Lizard Brain; it sends behavioral signals to us, which are strong and seemingly involuntary.

In developed countries, where human survival needs have become less imperative, some say that the lizard brain now focuses more on our "social survival." This may push that automatic, emotional reaction to an event that seems socially threatening, such as an event that threatens a relationship, our identity, or our freedom. In mediation trainings, a colleague will often ask whether parties are experiencing reactions from their lizard brain, because those unconscious reactions are often much more difficult to work through than others (Dugan, M. & Dunne, T., 2002).

HOW CAN COMMUNICATION HELP WITH CONFLICT MANAGEMENT?

Have you ever heard people say that a conflict or a problem was caused by a "communication breakdown"? Of course, communication does not really break down, but many people find that saying the right thing at the right time is not a skill that we are born with; we have to work hard at it and some people are better at this than others are. In our classes, we often discuss with students the fear that people have about communicating. Depending on the situation, we all find ourselves anxious about communicating. Asking your supervisor for a raise, confronting your friend about substance abuse, or sitting down and really discussing your financial situation with your spouse may be situations that give us pause. However, with the right tools, we can have some confidence that, even though we are afraid or anxious, we will still do some good with our communication. When we talk about *communication competence*, we are referring to communication skills. Scholars have defined communication competence as communicating in both an appropriate and an effective manner (e.g., Trenholm & Jensen, 2007). When we say "appropriate," we are focusing on the situation and the kind of communication that will be accepted. For instance, the way that you communicate with your family is probably different from the way that you communicate with your friends, which is probably different from the way that you communicate at work or school. Different situations are affected by both the context and the cultural and social backgrounds of the people involved.

When we say "effective," we are focusing on how, and whether, the communication that people use helps them to accomplish their goals. When they are communicating, people have many different kinds of goals; sometimes they may have multiple goals at the same time. Imagine that you would like to approach your neighbors about asking them to try to quiet their dog at night. You have been having some trouble getting to sleep because of the barking and you are hoping that by talking to your neighbors, you will be able to sleep better in the future. So, one main goal that you have for communicating is to effectively convince your neighbors to quiet their dog at night. However, since your neighbors are people with whom you may interact often, you also want to make sure that you do not offend or upset them with your request since that would make your day-to-day life more difficult. Thus, you have another goal—that of maintaining a good relationship with your neighbors. Several other goals could also be involved in this kind of conversation; in order for your communication to be competent, you need to recognize all of your goals and try to effectively accomplish all of them.

Having an understanding about competent, or skillful, communication is important for mediators because, in many ways, a mediator can become a type of *communication coach*. When two or more people have trouble communicating with each other, and are unable to manage their conflict, it is the mediator's task to help them effectively communicate with each other. A mediator's understanding of emotions and their effect on communication, and of appropriate and effective communication, can help parties understand each other better and hopefully resolve their conflict.

SKILL BUILDING ACTIVITIES

After reading through this chapter, take some time to work through a couple of skill building activities that should help you understand the nuances and feelings associated with conflict.

1. **Write a case study:** Describe either a conflict that you have been involved with or one you have observed. Follow a structure in which you, a) describe the conflict generally—e.g., what is it about? Who are the players? What is specifically disputed? b) describe each party's perspective in more detail—e.g., what was each party feeling? What did they say? What was their "take" on the conflict? Take one or two pages to write out your case study and then share it with others in this course.

2. **Emotional Charades**: Use the list of feeling words in a game of charades. Write each feeling on a separate card and put them all in a hat. Then, in a group of your colleagues, try to act out each feeling without saying what the feeling is. You can allow both verbal and non-verbal communication as long as you do not mention the feeling or try to use synonyms of the feeling. This will help you practice both your own clear communication skills and your interpretation of others' emotions.

3

Why Mediation?

The nature of conflict is such that it inherently affects our relationships because it involves interdependent individuals; people work together to make conflict and manage conflict. That is one reason that mediation is so appropriate for many kinds of conflict. Rather than simply focusing on the fair distribution of resources or punitive measures, mediation focuses on helping participants to work out their problems interdependently—like they started. By working together, many people who go through mediation find that they not only come up with an acceptable resolution to their conflict, but they learn to repair their relationships and work more effectively with their conflicts in the future.

Not all conflicts are appropriate for mediation, but a wide variety of conflicts will benefit from mediation. For example, many community dispute resolution programs specifically focus on handling family disputes (such as parent-teen conflicts or divorce settlements), neighborhood disputes (problems with noise, homeowners associations, or other neighborhood rules and regulations), tenant-landlord disputes, assault and battery disputes, or temporary restraining orders. Many schools now have dispute resolution programs that encourage mediation for students in conflict over relational issues, sharing, roommate problems, grade disputes, or organizational conflicts within the school. Mediation can often help the parties in these disputes learn to work together better, repair relationships with each other, and learn to handle conflict in the future more productively.

However, even though mediation may help people work through their issues, some people are initially resistant to mediation for a number of reasons. For instance, one of the parties in the dispute may not feel that they are responsible for the dispute. We have often heard people say that "it's their problem, not mine" when suggesting mediation (see activity 3.1). Another issue is that one or more parties do not believe that mediation will work even after they have been told about the process. They may feel that they have "tried everything" and that bringing in a third party "is not going to help." Finally, some people feel embarrassed about the conflict, or they believe that the conflict should be private and they do not want to bring in a third party.

Sometimes, even after parties agree to try mediation and the process has started, they may want to stop the process. There are several reasons for this. Some people may not trust the other party and feel that, even in the mediation, the other party does not in good faith want to work things out. Others may fear that the mediation will not be held confidential—they may not trust the other parties to keep the process a private one. Still others may feel that going through mediation means they have to compromise, and they are not willing. These individuals often want "their day in court" and believe that a judge, jury, district attorney, or other authority will see their evidence and make sure that the other party is "punished."

Case management is the term used to describe the entire process of mediation. This includes getting the parties to buy into the process, scheduling the mediation, assigning the mediators, and following up with parties after the mediation has finished. "Case managers" have very important jobs. They bring the parties to the table, help the parties understand how mediation can benefit them, and help them to trust that the process will work for them. In some cases, the person who mediates the dispute is also the case manger; but in other cases, one person starts the process and others mediate the process and follow through.

When the case management process starts, usually someone involved in the dispute who believes that mediation would be appropriate approaches the case manager. Most of the time, one of the parties approaches a case manager and suggests using mediation services to help resolve a dispute. In some cases, all of the parties will approach a case manager together and ask for mediation services to help them resolve a dispute. In still other circumstances, the parties are referred to the case manager by another organization that believes that mediation can help them.

If one party approaches a case manager wanting mediation, it is the case manager's job to ascertain the nature of the dispute; the case manager will also explain the mediation process so that the person understands what to expect. Then, the case manager must approach the other parties in the dispute to ask them if they would be willing to use mediation. Again, the case manager must inform them about the mediation process and get an idea about the nature of the dispute from their perspective. However, when approaching parties, the case manager also needs to get "buy-in" from the parties—in other words, convince them that mediation is an appropriate action to take. In our experience, if one party has suggested mediation, most of the time the other parties will be open to it as well. Often, these parties realize that the person with whom they are in conflict is genuinely willing to work through a dispute when they learn that mediation is being proposed; thus, they are willing to work through it as well.

It is important for the case manager to inform the parties about the mediation process, such as telling them that it is voluntary, confidential, and that the mediators will not make a decision about a dispute. The process is centered on the parties and only helps them come to a resolution. However, it is also important for the case manager to listen closely to all the parties and validate their perspectives. Sometimes parties really need to "vent" about their perspective in a conflict, and the case manager has to be willing to listen while still remaining neutral (see Chapter Five for some tips on maintaining neutrality). Other parties feel as though they are "victims" and that they will never be able to resolve their dispute fairly. In these cases, the case manager must remind the parties that conflict is interdependent; both parties have important interests that should be heard; and both parties should be open to hearing about the interests of the other. Often, these parties need to be reassured about the process and understand that no one will force them into an agreement they do not believe is right for them.

Finally, it is important for case managers to demonstrate the value of mediation to the parties. Without lecturing them on all of the positive aspects of mediation, case managers focus on what they believe the parties need to hear in order to get them to the table. Understanding the value of using mediation is paramount for a good case manager; and being able to articulate the value to others is an important aspect of bringing people to the mediation table.

THE VALUE OF MEDIATION

Mediation is a valuable process for everyone involved. Even when participants do not come to a resolution, they often find that going through the mediation process helps them to understand themselves and others better. It also gives them skills for managing future conflicts more effectively than they have in the past. In this section, we will highlight what we have seen demonstrated as valuable outcomes of mediation. We certainly cannot imagine every positive aspect of mediation that people have experienced, but we will outline many of those that repeatedly come up with people who have participated in mediations with us.

First, mediation helps many people build their self-esteem. While it may seem odd that going through a process of conflict resolution could help build self-esteem, some people feel that they have never been totally heard, and others have never felt validated for whom they are and what they stand for. Individuals who have gone through life feeling judged and ridiculed may take longer to trust the mediation process than others. However, once they discover that both the mediators and the other party will hear them, thus validating their perspective, they begin to realize that each individual perspective is valuable and important. The mediation process is empowering for those who feel that they are being heard for the first time. Others learn to recognize multiple perspectives and understand that they should not feel threatened or defensive when the perspectives of others are different from their own. The process of mediation demonstrates that there is no right and wrong way of believing or of handling things; there are just different ways of perceiving things, and we need to work together to understand that.

Mediation also helps people understand how to take responsibility for their own lives and decisions. Participants in mediation begin to realize their interdependent nature and understand that their decisions have outcomes that affect others. Because mediators do not interfere or make decisions for people, they are empowered to understand both how their actions have affected others in the past (through active listening and open understanding) and how much power they have to work out a shared solution with another party. Mediation gives participants the ability to not only have their needs met, but also to accept someone else's needs that are different from their own.

Because mediation focuses on helping people communicate better with one another about their conflicts, it also has the added benefit of helping people learn communication skills that they can use in other situations. Many people who participate in mediation find themselves better able to handle other conflicts in their lives because they learn to listen better and communicate their needs more clearly. Mediation, therefore, helps people build and maintain relationships through good communication practice. It helps people build understanding, and reduces their tension and anxiety surrounding conflict. Many people, who view conflict as something to be feared, leave mediation understanding that conflict helps us learn more about others, and ourselves. This gives them hope that future conflicts can be worked out.

Mediators need to be able to build an argument about the value of mediation—both as case developers (getting people to the table) and within the mediation session as well (if parties start to question whether this process will really work). An important skill for any mediator is being able to talk articulately about why mediation is a valuable exercise. We encourage you to practice this skill by working through one of the following role-play exercises. If you have never taken part in a role-playing activity before, you may want to look at Appendix A for some tips on successful role-plays.

ACTIVITY 3.1
CASE DEVELOPMENT ROLE-PLAY EXERCISE

For the case development role-play exercise, you and one other person will take turns playing the role of a mediator who has been contacted by one party who would like to mediate. After talking with this party, you will contact the person with whom your party is in conflict, and try to convince that person to mediate. You will also schedule a time when both parties will be able to meet.

Mediators have three specific goals in this exercise. First, contact and inform the second party about mediation. Make sure that person understands the mediation process. Second, explain the benefits of mediation to the party (and remember to keep party one's information confidential). Third, once you have convinced the party to mediate, you will need to schedule a time to meet with the first party.

Mediator/Case Developer

A female student who lives in the dorms at a local university has just approached you. This is her first year on campus and she has been having some problems with her roommate. When the student approached the Resident Assistant about the problems, the R.A. suggested mediation. The student has told you that she is very serious about school and really needs time and space in her room to study and rest. However, the student is upset with her roommate because she claims that the roommate is loud, incredibly messy, and constantly has friends over. The student is particularly annoyed that the roommate entertains her romantic partner in the room quite often and this is distracting.

Now, you need to call the student's roommate and convince her to attend mediation.

You have been given Monday afternoons, Tuesday evenings, all day Friday, and anytime over the weekend as acceptable times for mediation.

Roommate

This is your first year in the dorms on the university campus and you are really excited about the new experience of being at a university and out of your parents' house. Everything has been great—you have made many friends and you have a great romantic partner with whom you spend a lot of time. It is important to you that you have a university experience in which you make many connections with new friends and colleagues. The only problems you have had are with your roommate who seems really uptight and dull. You cannot get your roommate to have fun with you, and she is always complaining about you being in your room—but it is your room too! You actually tried to transfer to another room with a different roommate, but housing services told you that there were no available rooms. It is annoying to be dealing with this; and, frankly, dealing with your roommate seems to take away from the new social life that you are developing. Now, you get a call from Mediation Services.

4

The Mediator
as Communication Coach

By now, you have an understanding of the nature of conflict and know why mediation is an appropriate method to use for conflict resolution in certain cases. The task of a mediator is both challenging and rewarding. It is a wonderful feeling to be able to help people come to an understanding about each other and their problems. However, because people usually do not come to mediation until the conflict becomes irresolvable for them, being a mediator is also a very challenging and difficult role. In this chapter, we explore the different facets of the mediator's role. In addition to explaining the different aspects of the role, we will also challenge you to work through some difficult issues associated with maintaining the role of a mediator. You will also learn about, and work with, some of the tools that you can effectively use to coach people in conflict about their communication practices.

Assuming the role of a mediator is a lot like being a coach or manager. The mediator in a dispute must keep everyone in the room engaged with each other and the topic. Also, the mediator must keep the parties on the same page with respect to goals and desired outcomes—such as finding a peaceful resolution to their conflict. The mediator must understand every facet of the process, must ensure that all of the participants know the rules of engagement, and must make sure that the participants are willing and motivated to follow the rules. The mediator is more than a technician or a coaching specialist; as a communication coach, the mediator must know how to communicate to all participants in the language of the overall mediation process, as well as understand each phase of the mediation encounter. Thus, the mediator makes sure that ground rules are established and followed, that participants stay engaged and focused, and that participants are communicating in the most competent or skillful way that they can with each other.

Keeping the participants/disputants concerned about more that just their side of the argument makes the mediator's role slightly different from a coach. Having the participants understand the *interdependent* relationship in which they are involved heavily influences the mediation process. Participants need to understand that they *need each other* in order to come to a resolution. The goal of mediation is not to engage in a zero-sum contest for one party to beat the other in a game or challenge. Thus, unlike a coach, the mediator does not encourage one side to "win" in a competition. Rather, the mediator coaches two or more participants in effective communication skills for managing their conflict; the mediator coaches them on how to *be a team,* not on how to compete as two or more separate teams. The ultimate goal is to settle the emerging issues causing the conflict and come to an agreement about how to handle the issues when the parties return to their respective environments.

Mediators become coaches when they help the disputing parties communicate with each other. Mediators listen to and analyze what the parties are saying about the conflict and about themselves; they help interpret the different meanings that can be understood from what the parties say. Mediators help the parties understand

---

Figure 4.1: Communication Skills for Mediators

Active Listening: Communicate to someone that you hear what he is saying. Use neutral language to reflect content and feelings back to the person by restating or summarizing what he has said (Chapter Four).

Focus on Interests, Not Positions: Try to move past individual assumptions and focus on each party's interests and needs in the mediation. Move away from "solution talk" in the first parts of the mediation and toward identifying interests. Asking *clarifying questions* can help to focus on feelings and needs (Chapter Four).

Caucusing: Provide a break in the mediation session to talk individually with parties or other mediators (Chapters Four and Five).

Reframing: Use neutral language to transform emotionally charged or threatening language so that it is easier to *hear.* Typically, a mediator will *summarize* a party's statements in a neutral fashion (Chapter Five).

Validating: Recognize and appreciate the actions of parties in the mediation. Use supportive communication to express understanding of the difficulty and importance of the process and your appreciation of the parties' participation (Chapter Five).

Maintaining Neutrality: Keep an open and sincerely interested attitude during mediation. Be careful not to take sides, or *appear* to take sides. Asking questions to foster your own and the other party's understanding will help communicate your sincerity and neutrality.

each other better by modeling competent communication behavior through reframing statements, questioning and validating, and helping the parties use these same communication behaviors to communicate with each other. In addition, the parties learn from this experience as they interact with each other and the mediator.

LISTENING

One of the basic techniques employed in mediation is effective listening skills. Effective listening encourages a participant to concentrate and be open to what another person is saying. "Active listening" is one form of effective listening, and mediators have to prepare the participants to follow their lead by modeling active listening from the beginning of the meeting. By following the mediator's model, the participants should begin to show nonverbal engagement when the other party is speaking. A person can demonstrate active listening in mediation by maintaining eye contact, leaning forward, expressing acknowledgement, nodding, and patiently waiting for the other party to finish.

From the beginning of a mediation session, the mediator uses the following methods to set the tone for active listening.

- Extensive introductions: This helps everyone understand who the mediators are, what the mediation session is about, what will happen, and reminds parties that mediation is a voluntary activity.

- Express thanks to the participants for their willingness to engage: It takes courage for the participants to come to a mediation session; acknowledging that from the start helps participants realize the importance of what they are doing.

- Express a set of listening guidelines, which will be the prevailing standard for the conversation: Being clear about the communication ground rules from the start is a great way to start the "coaching" session in effective communication.

- Demonstrate what is meant by active listening: During the session, the mediator models active listening for the parties. This helps them to see how active listening works, and they can appreciate what it feels like to be listened to—which is vital for a good mediation session.

In mediation, listening is more than comprehending information. Participants often find themselves in mediation because *they believe that they have not been heard*. They may have said these words repeatedly; but until each participant perceives that they have been heard by the mediators and by the other participants, the mediation cannot effectively go forward. Active listening ensures that not only do participants comprehend information, but also that they respond to the other parties in a way that demonstrates that they have heard and comprehended them.

Activity 4.1: Communicating Listening

Think about the different ways that we can communicate with each other. How could you demonstrate that you have really heard and understood someone if you were in each of the following situations?

Sitting across from each other

On the telephone with each other

Emailing each other

Text messaging each other

Standing next to each other (but not facing each other)

PROVIDING STRUCTURE

The mediation is a structured conversation between disputing parties, facilitated by the mediator who acts as a manager/coach. The mediator's first responsibility is to ensure equity in the process. While strict equality is not always possible in a conversation or dialogue, the mediator strives to balance the communication opportunities available for each person involved in the dispute as much as possible. Each participant will have an opportunity to express their version of what transpired in the past that brought the issues to the point of dispute. The content or formal statement of indispensable information, according to the respective parties, allows the parties to state the crucial matters that began and contributed to the development of the disagreement. The more opportunities parties have to *be heard* in this process, the more likely they are to believe in and trust the process.

Part of the *structure* of the mediation session has to do with the feelings that are evoked. The feelings that surface in disputes are often as important as the other content issues, and many times are more important. These issues are often overlooked by other dispute resolution processes. Because feelings are thought to be too subjective, not concrete enough, or not compensation worthy, they are omitted from other dispute resolution processes such as litigation or arbitration. However, as you probably remember from Chapter 2, feelings are an important part of how people deal with conflict. This is one of the unique and empowering aspects of mediation, which is why it is vital that a mediator make sure to always ask about, and help "unpack," the feelings that disputing parties are having throughout the mediation. Sometimes, just naming a feeling that someone seems to be having (e.g., "You seem to be feeling really frustrated about this") can help a party to really *be heard* and feel more comfortable going on with the mediation. When a person's feelings can be acknowledged and analyzed as part of the texture of the dispute, those feelings can be addressed and resolved. Communication about feelings is often therapeutic, and can help the disputant understand how their actions:

- Caused resistance in the other party
- Broke a bond of trust
- Made the actions of the other party seem personal
- Caused parties to stop communicating
- Contributed to anger and fear in the relationship

Opening up the pathways of communication to include the feelings that have surfaced since the dispute began can lead to one of the most curative and corrective lines of communication in the mediation process. Developing this pathway without appearing to be invasive or overly psychoanalytic (remember, the mediator is not a counselor) may allow secondary benefits to emerge, including repairing a relationship that was formerly positive and personal. Parties will begin to take responsibility for their part in the dispute and be more willing to work with each other.

CASE 4.1
THE HO'OPONOPONO

Ho'oponopono is an ancient Hawaiian technique meaning "to make things right," and has been used within family systems to resolve domestic issues (Kanahele, 1986, p. 154). The procedure was entered into to help recreate the *LOKAHI* (unity) that is essential to Hawaiian cultural practice. This holistic social-cultural transaction helped to:

- Bring like and unlike things together in unity and harmony
- Set things right by successive stages of confession, repentance, and reconciliation
- Restore a context of peace

In a recent high profile case involving a dispute over an unlawful removal of artifacts, a federal judge suggested the *Ho'oponopono* process as a way to address the issue of proper transference of the artifacts and to heal the rift caused by their removal from their original burial site (Da Silva, 2006).

Native Hawaiian culture has rich spiritual and family integrity traditions that put a premium on restoring harmony to the family unit when there is a rift.

> If the Hawaiian saw a world in which all things are interrelated, linked as in a vast "cosmic grid," then we can reasonably conclude that even extreme opposites are linked as if they are two sides of the same reality... When the whole is viewed as a whole, then all idiosyncrasies and irregularities shown by individuals will disappear... attaining a dynamic and feasible balance between the two extremes (Kanahele, p. 155).

The leadership in the family has a duty to find a way to help the group get back to its essential functions, continuing the community enterprises that sustain economic viability and cultural harmony. The role of gathering critical dispute feedback as practiced by the *Haku* (managing director) of *a ili ohana* (autonomous extended family grouping):

The abiding features of the *Ho'oponopono* process highlight restoring civic cooperation to achieve the major goal of maintaining cultural integrity. Ancient practice might have had the whole of the community come together. Later, it was more likely that the more immediate family members were involved, sometime excusing the children. The process is described below:

- Opening *pule* (prayer) and prayers any time they seem necessary.
- A statement of the obvious problem to be solved, or prevented from growing worse. This is sometimes called *kukulu kamahana* in its secondary meaning.
- The "setting to rights" of each successive problem that becomes apparent during the course of *ho'oponopono*, even though this might make a series of *ho'oponopono* necessary (*mahiki*).
- Self-scrutiny and discussion of individual conduct, attitudes and emotions.
- A quality of absolute truthfulness and sincerity. Hawaiians call this *oia'i'o* the "very spirit of truth."
- Control of disruptive emotions by channeling discussion through the leader.
- Questioning of involved participants by the leader.
- Honest confession to the gods (or God) and to each other of wrongdoing, grievances, grudges, and resentments.
- Immediate restitution or arrangements to make restitution as soon as possible.

- Mutual forgiveness and releasing from the guilt, grudges, and tensions occasioned by the wrongdoing (*hala*). This act of repenting, forgiving, and releasing embodies the twin terms, *mihi* and *kala*.

In modern Hawaii, *Ho'oponopono* techniques might find themselves more widespread on the islands. The uses of *Ho'oponopono* extend beyond disputes within families or conflicts over inheritances. The tenets of dialogue, mutual ownership of issues, restitution, and reconciliation can be applied to today's society in, and outside of, Hawaii. More and more, legal practice is using Hawaiian techniques as cross-cultural methodologies for alternative dispute resolution (Barkai, 1992; Shook, 1986; Wall & Callister, 1995).

1. How does the *Ho'oponopono* mirror the Western mediation practice that we discuss in this text? How does it differ?

   _____

   _____

   _____

2. The *Ho'oponopono* puts an emphasis on family and community involvement in disputes. Is that appropriate? Would it make sense to bring more people into a mediation session in the United States?

   _____

   _____

   _____

3. How might a person from Hawaii, who has used and valued the *Ho'oponopono*, react to being a part of a mediation session in the U.S.? As mediators, what concerns might you have about the cultural differences of parties if one party was more accustomed to the *Ho'oponopono* practice and the others were more accustomed to a litigation type of dispute resolution?

   _____

   _____

   _____

FOCUSING ON INTERESTS, NOT POSITIONS

In a groundbreaking bestseller about negotiation, Fisher, Ury and Patton (1992) describe the importance of focusing on interests, not positions, to reach a good negotiation result. The same is true in mediation. Because a mediator really helps the disputing parties effectively negotiate a resolution with each other, helping the parties to understand good negotiation techniques is important. Focusing on *interests* means that parties should focus on the *reasons* that they are in conflict. This is in direct contrast to focusing on *positions*, which means that parties focus on what they think should be the outcome.

Helping the parties explore the essential interests in question, as opposed to their respective positions on the issues, are basic and fundamental in finding resolution in mediation. However, it is not always easy to move parties away from stating, and standing steadfastly on, what they see as the facts that will help them win a case. Our collective social mindset is lodged in the judicial process (i.e., litigation) where facts, evidence, and proof establish blame and probable cause. In mediation, it is not necessary for the parties to *prove* their respective cases, so much as to successfully communicate that they think their interests and feelings are not being acknowledged and cared about. In doing so, mediation establishes a clear structure for participants to explore what brought them to this point in their conflict and provides them with a baseline of mutual understanding from which they can begin to work on a resolution. That the action of the other party made someone feel a certain way, or developed a sense in them that their interests were not being recognized, is not a *fact* as much as a definite *perspective* on the matter. These perceptions are neither right nor wrong; they simply help parties tell each other what they felt when they did not take the others' interests or feelings into consideration. Mediators help parties communicate their perceptions as well as help the parties understand that they are *perceptions* and not necessarily facts.

Interests, or needs, could be expressed as a curiosity about something, a concern, attention given to something, a quality or activity in which one feels they have a justifiable, ethical, equitable, economic, social, or cultural right to have recognized by another party. Feelings emerge around interests, and people often set themselves in a position to establish that they have a legal right to something, when what they are really establishing is that their perspective on the these issues should be heard and recognized as a consequence of a relationship they have, or would like to maintain, with the other party. Mediators should help parties discuss how actions of the other party helped develop the feelings and perspective they now hold rather than trying to bolster their position with what they feel are objective facts.

CASE 4.2
THE SILENT OBSERVER

In a neighborhood mediation program, a neighbor had been accused of harassing some children in the neighborhood. The children's mother said that her children were afraid of the man across the street because he stared at them and watched them when they were outside playing. They were so frightened of him that they refused to go out and play in front of their house or in the street. The mother called the police and the police visited the neighbor and ended up taking him away in a police car and formally charging him with alleged criminal action.

The district attorney, however, thought there might be a way to resolve this matter outside of the court system, and so he referred the neighbors to mediation. When the parties were at the mediation table, the mediator asked the mother why she was so concerned. She explained that the other party frightened her children, and she was concerned about their safety. She felt that his frequent observation of the children was threatening.

The mediator then asked the man what his concerns were. He was upset and scared because he did not understand what he had done that was frightening. He said that his wife had died three months ago, and that they didn't have any children or close friends. He was quite lonely and was many days in the house by himself. His only interaction with other people was to watch the children play in the street or in front of their yard that was across the street from his house. The man was eighty-three years old.

When the mother heard about this man's life, and understood that he did not intend to hurt her children, she dropped the charges against him, and then invited him to dinner so that he could meet her kids and get to know her family. He was overwhelmed and pleased with her invitation.

1. What about the communication between these parties contributed to the ultimate misunderstanding about the older man's intentions?

   _____

   _____

   _____

2. Why do you think it was so easy for the parties to resolve this dispute in mediation when it obviously was not easy for them before attending mediation? In other words, why did mediation work?

    _____

    _____

    _____

3. What were each parties interests in this case? What were their positions?

    _____

    _____

    _____

4. What could have been an alternate outcome to this situation if the case had indeed gone to court?

    _____

    _____

    _____

MAINTAINING CONTROL

The mediator must always be in control of the mediation session, and must, at all times, be aware of the communication behavior, both overt and passive, of the participants. Thus, in addition to modeling effective communication behavior, it is also necessary for the mediator to monitor the participants to watch for possible problems with their communication—part of being a good coach is helping to correct mistakes. There are times when one participant may utter mean-spirited statements about the other. This should be discouraged firmly and decisively. The mediator has the obligation of maintaining an atmosphere where discourse can flow freely. Setting the standard of communication with ground rules at the beginning of the session, and challenging the parties to stay within the standard at all times is a paramount duty of the mediator. At times, the mediator should choose to manage the process by interrupting it. There may even be cause to end the mediation if participants are not, in good faith, following the guidelines set for the mediation at the beginning. The latter is not a desired outcome; however, trying to continue a session that has lost its civility, its standard of fair play, or its focus on movement toward mutually beneficial outcomes is the most undesirable outcome. The situations that most often cause mediation to stop temporarily or terminally are:

- **Visible fatigue**: Mediation is an emotionally and physically tiring process and both mediators and participants may experience overwhelming fatigue during the session. Mediators need to be aware of both their own and the participants' levels of fatigue to prevent problems from occurring.

- **Inciting language**: Participants are often emotionally vested in the conflict that comes to mediation, and sometimes can "frame" their feelings or interests in a way that is hurtful to the other participant. Whether this occurs intentionally or not, the mediator needs to watch for this kind of language use and either reframe it immediately, or, if it is ongoing, stop the mediation process for a caucus or longer.

- **Uneven participant communication**: Mediators may find that some participants tend to dominate the session after a while. Making sure to halt this kind of inequity is important for a number of reasons. Many different things can cause participants to feel like they cannot communicate in mediation; it is the mediator's job to make sure that *everyone* is heard (not just the squeaky wheel). When participants are communicating unevenly, look for the following: communication *style* problems (competitive versus avoidant styles); social or economic power imbalances that make one party feel uncomfortable communicating with the other (socio-economic, gender differences, cultural differences, rank differences at work or age differences); a fear of being misunderstood (meaning that the party has not yet developed a trust for the process).

- **Violence or allusions to violence**: If there are any allusions to violence occurring during the mediation, the mediator needs to assess that potential problem before anything happens. The mediator either de-escalates the situation through caucusing or other communication, or ends the mediation. A general rule of all mediators is that we will not put ourselves in personal danger during a mediation session. While this is *extremely* rare, it is important to be prepared to protect yourself should anything happen.

- **Wholesale resistance to move ahead**: Sometimes parties are not prepared to go ahead with mediation. For whatever reason, the parties may not be open to working with the other party. In this case, if the mediator cannot convince the resistant party to be more open to the process, the mediation should be ended.

While mediators should always try to convince parties to revisit the ground rules and continue participation in the process, they need to maintain control of the process as well. When mediators feel that they have lost control of the process, they may suggest stopping the process. A mediator who perceives that there is a reason to stop the mediation process, has several alternatives to consider:

- **Take a break**: Take a recess, allow the parties to walk around or sit separately before reconvening. See if they can cool down or change their outlooks.

- **Caucus**: The caucus allows the mediator a time to recess and take each participant into a private session to talk about the issues blocking or preventing communication. Even if there is a determination that only one of the participants is in need of the private discussion, the other should be given equal time to talk to the mediator in private. This assures that the sense of equality of treatment is maintained.

- **Schedule a time to reconvene**: If the mediator determines that the parties have done as much as they can do in one session, schedule a follow-up session. This break might come because the issues are too complex to finalize in one session. This may be advisable if there is a sense that they have done all they can do psychologically and physically at this time, and that a break might help them reflect and return with fresh perspectives.

- **Stop the session and suggest a different mediator**: If you feel that the disputants have done all they can do with you as the mediator, but they might benefit by coming back to another session with a different process manager, then suggest this and take the lead in helping the participants schedule that new session.

- **Stop the session**: On the rare occasion that the mediation takes a turn away from productive interaction, or is tending toward other kinds of resistance and contentiousness, it may be warranted to suggest that the parties try a process other than mediation. *The moral victory that can be taken from the mediation encounter is that the mediator has modeled competent communication skills that may be remembered by the disputants.* This is a worthy goal; ending the process, if that is what should happen, should not be considered a failure.

Ideally, successful mediations occur when parties reach a mutual agreement. However, it is better for a mediation to go honestly through the process and end without a resolution than for a mediation to go through the resolution process when it perhaps should have been stopped. For instance, if the parties are not trusting in the process (the mediator can tell by their non-verbal signals or even verbally incendiary comments), but they go through the motions of putting together an agreement anyway, they are not likely to honor that agreement once they leave. They may still feel that they have been heard or they may still be angry with the other party. The mediator should not become so caught up in reaching a written agreement; the goal of helping parties understand how to keep resolving their differences is another part of the empowering nature of mediation. If people feel they are forced to come to a decision because of outside pressure, they are not likely to appreciate the written document or believe in the integrity of the process as much as they would if they came to the agreement of their own accord (with a little coaching help from their mediator).

CASE 4.3
THE DOG

In a neighborhood mediation program, two parties attended a mediation in which they wanted to work out a dispute about a barking dog. The parties who called the mediation program were a married couple who had a dog living with them. They were very fond of the dog and thought that it was generally well behaved. However, they had been having some trouble with their neighbor concerning the dog. Their neighbor was an older Vietnamese woman who lived alone and worked long hours at a salon she owned. She had made repeated complaints about the barking dog.

The mediators asked the married couple to talk about their concerns. They shared that they were upset about the way their neighbor was behaving. While their dog did bark sometimes, they felt that when their neighbor yelled profanity at the dog, this curtailed their ability to discipline and train the dog in the way they felt appropriate. They used positive communication and reward with the dog, and felt that their dog did not respond well to their neighbor's yelling.

When the mediators asked the Vietnamese woman to talk about her concerns, she explained that her neighbor's dog made her feel threatened in her own home. She often did her cooking outside in her backyard when she returned from work and found that the dog would bark ferociously at her through the fence. This made her feel unsafe while she was cooking. She also felt uncomfortable with what she perceived as her neighbors' lack of concern for her privacy and safety—they seemed more concerned about the dog.

The mediators had considerable difficulty working with the parties to move past their positions. The married couple maintained that they wanted their neighbor to stop yelling at their dog and apologize to them for her use of harsh language. They were unwilling to take any action on their part without receiving this assurance. The older woman maintained that the dog should be kept indoors after 8:00 p.m. (when she returned from work) in order to ensure that she could peacefully make her dinner in her backyard. She felt this was an easy solution and would not consider anything until she felt her neighbors considered what she felt was a reasonable request.

After two and a half hours of trying to help the parties move from positions to interests, the mediators needed a break. They called a caucus to talk to each other and to each party individually. When they talked with each other, one of the mediators suggested that there was a cultural issue at stake—both parties were making some basic cultural assumptions that were not being made clear to each other. As they talked with each of the parties individually, they found that, indeed, this was the case. The older woman felt disrespected because she was not being honored in her neighborhood as an elder member—something that she came to expect in her own cultural and social background. She felt that it would be a devastating loss of face for her to concede to any request if her own requests were not met. Also, she did not understand why her neighbors did not realize this assumption. The married couple was upset because they felt that they had worked hard on their relationship—helping the woman with yard work and assisting her with needed repairs—and that she was not respecting them by at least apologizing for such harsh language.

While the parties and mediators were too tired to continue with the mediation that evening, the mediators were able to talk with each party about the assumptions that they were making and to introduce them to the idea that the other party may not understand those assumptions. However, when the parties were called to schedule a follow up session, they revealed that they had been able to work out their differences on their own. Their exploration of assumptions during the mediation session helped them to work through some major differences in cultural understanding. Both parties felt like they had made significant progress in their relationship and in resolving their differences.

1. What about the communication between these parties contributed to their initial inability to resolve this dispute?

   _____

   _____

   _____

2. Why do you think it was so easy for the parties to resolve this dispute after leaving mediation than it was for them while they were in mediation? Do you think that the mediation failed when the parties left without a resolution?

_____

_____

_____

3. What were the interests of each party in this case? What were their positions?

_____

_____

_____

4. What could have been an alternate outcome to this situation if the case had not gone to mediation?

_____

_____

_____

Providing a Safe Place

What represents a safe environment for one person might be different for another; therefore, it is up to the mediator to determine what constitutes a safe environment in each mediation. Making the environment "safe" for mediation generally means keeping the environment free from violence (both physical and verbal), having respect for everyone in the mediation session; and, as a mediator, maintaining a neutral stance so that all parties feel they are equally heard. From the outset of the mediation, it is important to acknowledge to the parties what you can do to help make the environment safe for communication and what you might not be able to do.

The first aspect of safety is to define what constitutes a safe environment to you as the process manager. You set the standards for civility in communication; then you get the participants to agree that they will help maintain that standard. The mediator will establish how the participants are to communicate that they are not feeling safe, or if they feel the standards of communication are not being maintained by the mediator or by the other party. If those standards are not met, there has to be an agreement about what you will do as the mediator.

In general, a safe communicating environment has the following elements:

Mediation Preparation (Physical Space)

- The physical space should be at a neutral meeting space.
- The meeting should be conveniently accessible for each participant.
- If possible, take into account gender, culture, and language when choosing a mediator.
- The space should be well lit and in a safe area, especially for evening sessions. If there is a need to escort someone from the session, that should be provided.

During the Session (Emotional and Communication Space)

- There should be no yelling among participants.
- Participants will get to say what they feel they need to communicate without interruption.
- There will be no name-calling, cursing the other participant, or blaming the other person.
- All participants will be assured that their ideas and proposals will be given the same consideration as the other party's.
- Confidentiality is explicitly maintained. Each participant must sign off on any alteration of the confidentiality agreement.

However, even making sure that all of these criteria are met for a safe place, there are some things that a mediator cannot generally provide. The mediator is not usually a police official (although there are many great mediators who are also police), and cannot arrest or otherwise subdue an unruly person. However, the mediator should establish that any violent action will be cause for termination of the mediation, and any violence will be reported to the proper authorities.

The mediator, as a communication coach, has a challenging job. Nevertheless, through listening, providing structure, focusing on interests, maintaining control, and providing a safe space, the mediator can help disputing parties come together as a team to resolve their dispute.

CASE 4.4
ISRAEL AND PALESTINE

Israelis and Palestinians have been in major conflict for many years. Both are interested in living on the same land for religious and political reasons, but their conflict goes far beyond that. Because they have been in conflict for so long, parties on both sides have taken actions against each other that have significantly altered their ability to relate to one another.

Take some time to consider the interests and positions of Palestinians and Israelis. What are the main interests for each side of this conflict? What are the main positions for each side? You may find some basic information in the *Wikipedia* entry for Israel-Palestine conflict (www.wikipedia.com).

Global mediators have been trying to help resolve the disputes between Israel and Palestine for years, but they have been unsuccessful. What have been the major sticking points in these attempts (e.g., the Mid-East peace process)?

Now imagine that two student groups on a college campus are in dispute over a mural. The Muslim Student Organization wants to sponsor a mural portraying triumphant Muslim soldiers on the wall outside their student office. They believe that the military has been an important part of their history, and they want to demonstrate a positive image of Muslim military members. They believe this will help people understand the difference between military and terrorism.

However, the Jewish Student Organization is protesting the mural. Their argument is that, given the history of the Israeli-Palestinian conflict, the mural is threatening and should be considered hate speech. The Muslim Student Organization has countered by saying that the Jewish Student Organization is trying to censor them, which leaves them feeling as if their freedom is threatened.

Given the background of this conflict and the strong emotions surrounding it, work through the following questions:

1. How does the conflict between Palestine and Israel affect or influence the conflict with the student groups?

   _____

   _____

   _____

2. What ground rules might you anticipate needing in order to establish a mediation with the student groups? Which ground rules do you think will be most challenging for the parties to follow?

   _____

   _____

   _____

3. What are the interests of each student group? What are the positions? How do those interests and positions compare to the more global interests and positions of Israel and Palestine?

   _____

   _____

   _____

4. What specific safety concerns do you think the student groups might have? What would you do as a mediator to create a safe space?

   _____

   _____

   _____

SKILL BUILDING EXERCISE
RECOGNIZING INTERESTS AND POSITIONS

1. Imagine that two siblings are having a dispute about which of them should have their mother live with them. The first sibling, Sarah, thinks the other, Kim, should have Mom move in because Sarah has three children and is a single mother. Thus, she does not feel she has time to take care of her mother. Kim, however, feels Sarah should have Mom move in because Kim is paying for all of her hospital care and the nurse that visits her daily. What is Kim's position?
   a. That Sarah should have Mom move in with her because she is not paying for Mom's care.
   b. That Sarah's kids are not a good excuse for Mom not to move in.
   c. That the distribution of duties regarding Mom should be fair.
   d. That she is worried about Mom.

2. In the same situation, what is one of Kim's interests?
   a. Sarah should have Mom move in with her because she is not paying for Mom's care.
   b. Sarah's kids are not a good excuse for Mom not to move in.
   c. The distribution of duties regarding Mom should be equitable.
   d. She is worried about Mom.

3. Again, in the same situation, what is Sarah's position?
   a. She is worried about Mom.
   b. Kim should have Mom move in with her because she does not have to take care of three children by herself.
   c. Kim does not understand how hard it is for Sarah to get through the day even without taking care of Mom.
   d. The two sisters should contribute what they can, even if it is not equal.

4. Again, in the same situation, what is one of Sarah's interests?
   a. She is worried about Mom
   b. Kim should have Mom move in with her because she does not have to take care of three children by herself.
   c. Kim does not understand how hard it is for Sarah to get through the day even without taking care of Mom.
   d. The two sisters should contribute what they can, even if it is not equal.

5

The Mediator
as Communication Model

While one role of the mediator is that of communication *coach*, another is that of communication *model*. While the coach directs and sometimes creates the right environment for mediation, the model should serve as a reminder of how we need to behave in the environment. The mediator is the model of effective communication during the mediation session. Several techniques will be demonstrated throughout the mediation session and discussed in this chapter. Each of these techniques are communication tools that not only effectively structure the mediation, but also model how we hope the parties will talk with each other.

REFRAMING

When a picture or painting is reframed, a new perspective on the painting will emerge. The essential elements of the content remain the same, but alteration of the background or setting changes how one might perceive the content. The perspective of the speaker is understood fully through a series of reframes on a theme or thesis. The act of repeating oneself, hopefully achieves better understanding. That is not likely to have the same effect as offering different variations on the essential elements of an argument or perspective. In the process of reframing, not only does the receiving party give more information and a different perspective, but also the author of the perspective forces an expansion of the perspective. A more expansive take on issues brings matters of interest and feelings out in the open.

Mediators use reframing to *neutralize* statements that might be inflammatory or hurtful to the other party or the process. The mediators use this tool to help model effective communication. Thus, when a participant behaves in a way that does not model effective communication for the mediation process, such as blaming or accusing another party, focusing on positions instead of interests, using offensive or harsh language, or interrupting another party, the mediator can simply restate the original statement in a way that is effective. Consider the following examples:

Blame

My grades are slipping and I'm sleep deprived all the time and it's her fault because she plays this noisy racket in the apartment upstairs through all hours of the night!

Reframe

You are very concerned about your grades and your health and would like to make sure that you have more and better sleep.

Offense

She's just been so rude! She never acknowledges what I do around the house or helping with the kids. She just complains whenever she thinks I'm not doing enough.

Reframe

It is important to you that your work around the house be acknowledged and you are not hearing that acknowledgement from your spouse.

In both of these cases, the reframing statement begins to neutralize the original statement. In the "blame" situation, it is important for the mediator to focus on interests or needs rather than position. When one person blames another person, it has the effect of making attributions for another person's behavior (i.e., they imply that the other person had wrong intent). We will discuss this in more detail in Chapter Eight, but for now, it is important to recognize that by focusing on what is important to the first party (sleep), rather than the first party's assessment of her roommate's behavior, the mediator starts to neutralize the blame.

In the second example, the mediator also focuses on the party's need or interest. This party needs to be acknowledged for his contribution. However, labeling his spouse as "rude" is incendiary and might only make her feel indignant (especially if she felt that she had acknowledged his contribution but that he didn't *hear* it for whatever reason). By reframing this statement, the mediator helps to neutralize language that might have fostered divisiveness rather than understanding.

VALIDATING

We all need to have some sense that others understand what we are saying. One of the biggest frustrations that people experience in conflict occurs when one party uses words to describe feelings or interests that the disputing party does not clearly understand. We want to know that we have been heard—and not just heard, but understood in our own terms. Therefore, *validating* is a way to help each disputant confirm that there has been a cognitive moment when each party hears and comprehends what the other is trying to communicate. Mediators can model validation throughout the process by reminding participants how important it is that they have come to mediation, praising them for following ground rules in communication, and restating their most important statements so they know that the mediators have heard them.

At some point, parties are also encouraged to begin using validation in their own communication. The validating process for participants occurs when the mediator asks one disputant to listen to the other party without interruption. The listening party is then asked to repeat what was said using the same, or nearly the same, words. This is done for each of the participants and is repeated until the major and minor issues are communicated and validated. Restating others' statements may seem trivial outside of the mediation context. However, in a mediation, sometimes just hearing someone else say what a party wanted them to hear is the difference between whether that party works collaboratively toward a resolution or holds firm in a position. Remember that being *heard* and being *understood* are primary goals for any mediation; validation is integral to achieving those goals.

The validation process ensures that there has been, for the moments of this process, a complete and unimpeachable understanding of the parties' articulated interests and needs. This may be the first time that this understanding of the intellect, not just the passion, is confirmed. Going through this process helps achieve an unqualified degree of thoroughness and accuracy that satisfies the sense that each party knows the essence of the complaints of the other and also knows that the other party understands their own complaints and needs. While the mediation does not deal in right and wrong or unimpeachable evidence, the fullest picture of the dispute from all sides is achieved through reframing and mutual validating statements.

CAUCUSING

There are times when, as much forethought as we put into the environment and as much as we try to model effective and appropriate communication for the participants, something still seems wrong. As mediators, these are times when we need to call a caucus. A caucus is when mediators choose to meet individually with each party (and sometimes just with themselves if they are co-mediating) for a period during the mediation session.

A mediator may choose to caucus for a number of reasons, each of which is a signal that the parties and/or the mediator(s) need a break from working together. Reasons for taking a caucus might include:

1. One party seems to be dominating the mediation, and the mediator wants to give the other party a chance to speak.
2. The mediator senses that there is fear or a lack of trust between the parties that they cannot work through together.
3. Emotions are running too high and the mediator wants to give parties a chance to work through them individually.
4. Co-mediators want a chance to confer with each other.

When mediators choose to caucus, they need to explain to the parties that they would like to talk to each party individually and that they will hold these individual conversations confidential. Mediators should allow equal time for each party they are caucusing. Often, mediators are able to work through important issues during a caucus that parties then bring to the table. Some mediations may need several caucuses, whereas others will not need any. Some mediators like to use caucuses, while others do not. If you choose to use caucusing in a mediation, you will still want to maintain the same environment and modeling that you do in the whole session.

RESOLVING

Mediators are coaches and process managers; they are not involved in the process of positing specific resolutions for the parties. The parties are the players—the principals; they are encouraged, assisted, and provided a framework in which to find a solution. The process of mediation is interpersonally "empowering" in that the parties are offered a balanced and equitable playing field in which they can address concerns in the confines of a civil and safe process. The parties are offered tools for resolution, and they are asked to use the best thinking and analysis possible to achieve outcomes that are mutually beneficial and sustainable.

At times, the mediator will remind participants of issues they have previously raised. Other times, the mediator will assist in fleshing out the issues through clarification or alternative language phrasing such as reframing. However, the decisions about the specific actions, behaviors, conduct, or outcome is not the specific area of concern for the mediator. Even when helping to write the final agreement between parties, the mediator takes the role of a stenographer and not an authorized legal advocate. *The likelihood that the parties will stay in agreement is positively proportional to their perception of how much authority they had over making the actual agreement.*

EMBRACING A MODEL

While mediators will have their personal styles of mediation, they may also choose to operate in different *models* of mediation. For instance, some mediators meet with participants by themselves; whereas, other mediators work with a colleague and follow a co-mediation model. Some mediators use caucusing much more than others do. It simply depends on what makes each mediator comfortable. As long as the mediator is striving toward understanding among the parties, the model simply provides a comfortable structure for the mediator.

Table 5.1: Models of Mediation

Mediator Model	Number of Participants	Benefits
Single Mediators	There is an individual who acts as the proctor and facilitator of the process	Sole manager of process
Co Mediators	There are two proctors and facilitators of the process	Complementary management
Mediation Panel	There are more than two facilitators of the process	Balance culture, language, gender or other participant attributes
Caucus (Evaluative Mediation)	There is a single mediator or a panel	Expertise-based management

In addition to the various physical structures of mediations described in the table, mediators may also have different philosophies about the way they approach mediation. Each of these philosophies may be more or less appropriate depending on the situation. For instance, *facilitative* mediation operates with the belief that the parties can arrive at their own solution when provided with a structure for communication. *Transformative* mediation focuses on repairing the relationships altered or destroyed by the dispute. This process assumes that there is an empowering effect achieved through the mediation process. *Evaluative* mediation uses the mediator's expertise in a given field. The mediation goes on in individual caucusing and the final agreement is worked out as a negotiated agreement with each party making compromises until reaching a final agreement.

Because this text is geared more toward a general understanding of mediation, we will focus more on the facilitative and transformative models than on the evaluative model. We will also explore the ways in which single or co-mediation models may be useful as you learn more about your own mediation styles.

CASE 5.1
THE HEALING CIRCLE

Many traditions in Native American communities highlight the need for community, spirituality, and healing. One tradition, the community-healing circle, relates to conflict resolution. While this ceremony works well in group conflict resolution, it is also a medium for resolving sub-group and individual issues. Unlike the western ideal of rugged individualism, Native Americans often conceive of individual quarrels as a responsibility of the whole community to help resolve, as well as a responsibility the individual(s) accepts as a member of the community. Native Americans have a strong community pull toward conflict resolution.

The healing circle allows for a facilitator who is in every sense a co-equal to all others. While the facilitator is sometimes a leader in the community, everyone shares equally during the healing circle. The facilitator assumes the responsibility of getting the participants to stay within the collective conscience and goodwill of community. The person chosen is often considered an elder of the group—someone versed in group customs, history, and traditional practices. The role of the facilitator is not to assign blame, exact obedience, or assert specific knowledge, which is ecclesiastical or omniscient according to ancient or spiritual codes. Native Americans acknowledge that there are many ways of knowing, and that one should seek, and eventually, find and follow, the path that leads them out of conflict and into better understanding.

Healing circles may begin with a story that is a contextualizing reminiscence about the people in different times—both good or bad. This can be a way of tying the old with the new; the traditional or fateful incidents from the past that both show what the group has endured and how they have always overcome. The offering of dialogue is then extended to others, one by one, so that all members of the group are allowed to say what they need to relate. Each person is allowed to speak unfettered by interruption. There is no active hierarchy of gender or community roles while in the healing circle. Each person is honored as a substantial contributor based solely on group membership.

One of the major benefits of the healing circle seems to be the cathartic or eliminative nature of the exercise. While not all conflict is presumed to be harmful, some behavioral conflict is found to be dysfunctional when it inhibits maintaining community accord. The group's ability to work in proximity and harmony means the disputing individuals need to discuss how the offending conflict should be purged. Other benefits to this form of conflict resolution may be palliative in their effects. That is, a single solution may not emerge from the healing circle that provides for every contingency that arises in a session; however, there may be enough of a common understanding of a way to a better path to follow than has been previously understood. Allowing the disputants space to work toward the "cure" establishes a set of acknowledgments that lead to primary, or even temporal, agreements that put into place the best steps toward reestablishing community viability and harmony. Affirming disputants for their participation in the healing circle helps with face saving and asserts their willingness to help preserve community.

Native American communities use the healing circle to discuss important and critical issues in the community. This includes individual discord, group customs, practices, asset rights, asset management, health and wellness issues, etc. When approaching issues with Native American clients in a setting that is peripheral to their indigenous community, one should be sensitive to the issues of family and community. A mediation moderator who acknowledges an understanding of the centrality of familial ties and group practices takes a critical cultural assurance step toward engaging Native American clients.

Work with Native Americans in metropolitan communities might benefit from some understanding of the centrality of community and the equality of mutual cultural significance. It may be an unstated or understated expectation of Native American clients that they desire to be understood in these terms when asked to participate in mediation.

When misunderstanding occurs within a community, mediation sessions invoking some healing circle practices might be used complementarily to help diffuse issues. The healing circle structure, itself, can help supplant the notion that the mediation session is an across-the-table westernized negotiation discussion with an expectation of working toward a zero-sum outcome. Taking advantage of the circle and setting up the session so that parties feel they will be treated equitably and that the outcomes can allow for communal as well as individual repair is a benefit of conflict resolution through mediation or healing circles.

1. What similarities do you see between the healing circle and the practice of mediation? What are some differences?

   _____

   _____

   _____

2. What do you think about the act of bringing in an entire community to help facilitate a conflict among a few parties? In what situations do you think this would be appropriate? In what situations would it not be appropriate?

   _____

   _____

   _____

3. The community-oriented nature of the Native American culture is interdependent rather than the independent nature of a more Western culture. What aspects of an independent orientation to culture might help someone in the mediation process? What aspects of an interdependent culture would help someone in the mediation process?

   _____

   _____

   _____

Maintaining Neutrality

Maintaining neutrality may be one of the toughest, and most important, skills for a mediator to develop. A mediator must maintain complete neutrality—not take sides at all—in order for the participants to trust the mediation process and for it to work. However, that does not mean that a mediator must be a stoic. Mediators can do a number of things to help focus on being neutral outside parties without being *unfeeling* outside parties.

First, a mediator must maintain a true openness and curiosity toward all participants in mediation. Come to the mediation understanding that you have your own biases and perspectives on the world, but also understanding that those biases and perspectives are limited. Be open to anything—including the possibility that your perspectives may be inaccurate or constrained. As mediators, we have the wonderful opportunity to learn more about others and about ourselves during the process. Always be open to that kind of learning.

Mediators need to be careful that they do not make assumptions about the parties. Sometimes, because of our own experiences, we may believe that we understand why the parties act as they do; or we may think that we know what the parties should do in order to resolve a particular dispute. However, it is important to check these assumptions and remember that a mediator is just a communication and process coach. Rather than bring mediator opinions into the process, take the opportunity to learn why participants feel as they do, and why they believe a certain way is appropriate to resolve their dispute.

Second, a mediator must be aware of certain "trigger points" that they might have during conflict. Recognizing our own biases and understanding that certain things might threaten our ability to maintain neutrality helps us understand our own feelings during the mediation and makes it possible for us to make sure that we are modeling effective communication. For instance, a mediator who is a dog lover might find himself not appreciating one party's perspective because that party does not understand how dogs are trained. However, it is not the mediator's place to educate the party, and it is not appropriate for the mediator to take sides. Recognizing that this is a trigger point may help the mediator to understand how to better work through mediations that involve dogs in the future, or to not take on those kinds of mediations (for more insight, see trigger point exercise at the end of this chapter).

Recognizing our cultural biases and understandings about the world can be difficult. We construct our social worlds though our interactions and our communication; thus, we often favor our cultural leanings, because those are the people with whom we interact. All mediators should take time to consider their respective cultural backgrounds and the ways in which they daily interact with their world to understand how these cultural biases might influence the mediation. Take some time to think about whom you interact with—and whom you do not. Think about the people in your neighborhood, your workplace, your school, and your family. Do all of you share traits or perspectives? What is different among you? What is similar? Are there people with whom you do not interact much? If so, who are they? What beliefs or stereotypes might you have about them (whether they are positive or negative)?

As you work through the case studies at the end of this chapter, carefully consider the questions in the previous paragraph to see if your answers might help you learn more about yourself as a mediator.

CONCLUSION

The role of a mediator is complex, but a mediator's goal is simple: help the parties to understand each other better and hopefully resolve their dispute. In this chapter, we have discussed the importance of the mediator acting as a communication model by demonstrating reframing, validation, embracing a model, and maintaining neutrality. Now, take some time to work through the case studies and discuss how to effectively use these skills.

CASE 5.2
EXPELLED FROM SCHOOL

Mark, a thirteen-year-old boy with learning disabilities, was kicked out of school because he let some other students into his special ed teacher's room without her permission. Apparently, the teacher had trusted the student with keys to her classroom so that he could bring some supplies back to the room while the class was in the gym. But when the teacher came back to the classroom, she found the classroom in disarray with graffiti on the chalkboard and valuable supplies stolen.

Mark was asked to attend victim-offender mediation with his teacher so that they might work out a plan for restitution of the stolen supplies. During the mediation, the mediators first asked Mark to talk about his experiences since being expelled so that the teacher could hear what it had been like for him. Due to his expulsion, Mark was placed in another school; however, they had no programs for children with learning disabilities. He told the mediators and the teacher that he felt very isolated and lonely. He communicated that he felt badly about his past actions, and that he felt hopeless at how those actions had affected him in school. When he had let the other kids into the teacher's classroom, he had done so from peer pressure; he had learned from this experience that succumbing to peer pressure was not worth it.

The mediators then asked the teacher to share her perspective about the situation. The teacher was initially furious at what the boy did because she had tutored him and helped him, and she felt betrayed; she had trusted him, and when he did not act in a trustworthy way, she felt she had been deceived. She was angry and did not initially want to come to mediation. However, upon hearing Mark's story, the teacher changed her approach. She was able to see that Mark was in an unfortunate situation, and that rather than being punished for this event, he might be able to learn from it. She suggested that the mother drive him to his old school, where the teacher would tutor him and have him help the other students every Tuesday and Thursday afternoons for two months. If he did that faithfully, then she would ask the principal of the school to reinstate him and put him back in the classroom. When everyone agreed, the boy hugged the teacher.

1. What were Mark's interests in this mediation? What were the teacher's interests?

   _____

   _____

   _____

2. The teacher did not initially want to attend mediation. If you had been the case manager in this situation, what would you have said to encourage her to come?

   _____

   _____

   _____

3. Do you think that the teacher did the right thing? What risks did the teacher take in agreeing to have Mark work with her and her students as restitution?

   _____

   _____

   _____

CASE 5.3
FATHER-DAUGHTER PERSPECTIVES

After a father had called the police about his daughter's behavior several times, the family was referred to mediation to see if they might be able to work out some of their concerns. Present at the mediation were both parents and their sixteen-year-old daughter.

When the parents and teen were in the room together, the mediator asked the parents what their concerns were and what they wanted to get out of the mediation. The Vietnamese father said that his daughter belonged in a foster home or in Juvenile Hall where they would make her obey and punish her for disobeying. The European-American mother agreed with her husband that their daughter was difficult. The mediator realized that there was a strong power difference between the two parties and feared that the daughter might not feel comfortable talking with her parents present. Therefore, the mediator asked the parents to leave the room so that she could talk to the daughter privately. While the parents were in another room, the mediator asked them to write down all the *positive* things that they felt about their daughter.

When the mediator met with the daughter privately, she shared that her father was autocratic and that he gave harsh orders to her. She felt that he would never listen to her although she tried very hard to communicate with him. Their fights sometimes got so intense that her father called the police on her with accusations of harassment or theft (if she left taking a car). After the conversation, the mediator asked her if she was willing to talk to her dad with the mediator's help and tell him how she felt about him and his attitude towards her. She said that she was willing.

The mediator then talked to the parents without the daughter and asked them if they would be willing to share concerns directly with their daughter. The mediator explained to the parents how their daughter wanted to talk to them and hoped that they would listen. The mediator worked with the father during this caucus session to show him how to effectively communicate with his daughter, so that she could understand how he felt and how discouraged he was about trying to raise a daughter in this country. The mediator focused on helping the father with reframing and focusing on interests and needs.

When the daughter and parents were in the same room, the mediator asked the daughter to share one of her concerns with her father. She said, "Don't call the police on me. I am not a criminal. Couldn't we just sit down and talk." The father listened and then, out of the blue, when it was his turn to share, he said "I want you to forgive me for the way I treated you as a child." The daughter responded, "Dad, I have already forgiven you." The father broke down in tears and she hugged him. It was a very emotional time.

The agreement in the end was that the father agreed to talk to his daughter in the way that the mediator had coached him in using active listening and focusing on interests. The daughter would do the same to work out their disagreements by listening to her parents. They all left hugging each other, which was very different from the way they came in. The mediator told them that if they had any more difficulties to contact her and she would be glad to work with then again. Not surprisingly, they did not contact the mediation center again.

1. At the beginning of this mediation, the father was ready to send his daughter to a foster home. What changed?

    _____

    _____

    _____

2. Do you think that the mediator made the right call by going to a caucus so early in the mediation? What do you think would have happened if the mediator had let the parents and daughter share some concerns together before going to a caucus?

    _____

    _____

    _____

3. How could cultural or social background have influenced this conflict and the ultimate mediation process?

    _____

    _____

    _____

SKILL BUILDING EXERCISE 1
REFRAMING AND RESTATING

For each of the following statements, imagine that you are a mediator who has heard one of the participants say this statement during the mediation so that the other participant can hear it. Underline what you feel are the most important parts of each statement to reframe. As a mediator, please write out what you would say so that you: 1) make sure the offending participant knows that you have heard him/her; 2) the statement is reframed to repair/protect the feelings of the targeted participant.

1. *(Participants are Roommates)*

   There are dirty dishes and trash all over the room—she is a slob! How am I supposed to live with someone who obviously does not respect her environment?

   _____

   _____

   _____

2. *(Participants are neighbors)*

   Look, they are tree-huggers! They won't do the required maintenance on that tree in their yard because they can't handle cutting off a branch. It looks terrible and the seeds get stuck in my lawn mower.

   _____

   _____

   _____

3. *(Participants are neighbors)*

   Her children are running around like little devils all day and into the night! What kind of parent lets their children stay out so late and be so loud?

   _____

   _____

   _____

4. (*Participants are colleagues*)

    He just doesn't get anything done! I know that those people are generally kind of lazy, but if you're gonna have this kind of job, you've got to do the work!

    _____

    _____

    _____

SKILL BUILDING EXERCISE 2
WORKING THROUGH TRIGGER POINTS

As mediators, we need to be concerned about maintaining neutrality during the mediation session. While this can be difficult, one thing that can help is to learn what "triggers" might prevent us from being neutral in a mediation. Take some time to work through the following questions. These should help you identify personal assumptions and values that might act as trigger points.

1. What characteristics do you value in others? With what kind of people do you like to spend your time?

    _____

    _____

    _____

2. What characteristics concern you about others? For instance, what characteristics about others would keep you from wanting to be friends with them, or wanting to work with them?

    _____

    _____

    _____

3. Who, in our society, has *power*? Have they earned that power? How should they use it?

    _____

    _____

    _____

4. For those in our society who do not have power, what are acceptable ways for them to try to get more power?

   _____

   _____

   _____

5. Describe your ideal conversation. How are people communicating? How are they behaving?

   _____

   _____

   _____

6. After going through the previous questions, can you think of characteristics, behaviors, or situations that might cause you to lose a neutral position? What might those be?

   _____

   _____

   _____

As you conclude this exercise, remember that the more you are aware of your trigger points and assumptions, the more likely you will act neutrally and fairly in mediations. Something that is a possible trigger does not necessarily have to cause you to lose neutrality, but the fact that you have identified it can help you recognize and manage your own behavior in mediations.

6

The Mediation Introduction and Process Overview

This chapter provides an overview of the process of mediation—specifically the "introduction" part of mediation. Because overviewing the mediation process is typically part of the introductory statement, we will also go over each stage of the mediation so that you know what to expect. At the end of the chapter, you will have the opportunity to write out your own "cheat sheet" to help you go through the introduction and practice with each other.

In most mediations, the first session is also the first time the mediators and parties meet each other. In some cases, both parties may know the mediator before the first meeting; however, even in those cases, the introduction to the meeting serves to *set the tone* for the rest of the mediation. In the introduction, it is not only important for the mediators and participants to exchange names and niceties, but also for the mediator to effectively explain how the mediation process works and what will be expected of both the parties and the mediator.

SETTING THE TONE

Mediation is an interpersonal activity. The parties and the mediators are interdependent in that everyone needs to cooperate with each other in order for the process to be successful. Thus, it is important to begin the mediation in a friendly and cooperative manner. All mediators will have their own unique styles in terms of framing the mediation; however, several general aspects of the first part of the introduction will help set a cooperative tone.

First, introduce yourself (along with your co-mediator if you have one) in a way that makes you feel comfortable and makes clear how you would like to be addressed (for instance, we mostly ask to be addressed by our first names to make the mediation more casual). Then, ask the parties to do the same. Refrain from asking them to talk about why they are there or about their conflict at this point—you will have plenty of time to talk about that soon enough.

We often find that it is nice to offer words of encouragement immediately after introductions. It is not easy to make the decision to come to mediation, and it takes a strong person who is truly willing to cooperate to come to the table when he or she is having difficulty with a dispute. It is helpful to validate this action right at the outset and let the parties know that they are doing a great thing by *even showing up* to the table. This kind of validation should help set the tone of the mediation and remind the parties that they are doing good work and will continue to do so throughout the mediation. It also helps to remind them that they, and not the mediator, will be doing the work toward understanding and resolution. The mediator only shepherds this process.

Ensuring Voluntary and Confidential Communication

It is important to remind participants during the introduction that mediation is both a voluntary and confidential activity. Specifically, individuals should not be forced to attend mediation. Although many times individuals are given strong incentives to attend mediation, such as offering to delay a court appearance or citation if the individual chooses mediation, individuals must still make the decision to attend with free will. Some institutions that offer mediation have individuals sign a document that assures that they are attending a mediation session voluntarily.

Making sure that individuals are participating in mediations voluntarily is important, because it makes it much more likely that they are open and willing to follow the process of mediation. They will be more willing to follow ground rules and listen to the coaching of their mediators, and they will feel more empowered as they participate in the process if they are volunteers rather than if they are forced.

Further, mediations are confidential events. One of the ways mediators can assure a "safe" communication environment is to make sure that individuals know that what they say does not leave the mediation session. Mediators will hold all of their communication and observations confidential, and participants should agree to hold all of their communication and observations confidential as well. Generally, individuals feel freer to talk about their personal interests when they believe they are doing so in a private and confidential circumstance rather than a public one (e.g., Petronio, 2000).

In the state of California, mediators are protected by a confidentiality clause, which assures that they will not be subpoenaed into court to talk about a confidential mediation session.

> A mediator cannot be used as a witness or be called to testify in any manner in a civil court or non-criminal legal proceedings. A mediator may be called to testify about matters related to criminal endeavors if subpoenaed by the District Attorney. In such an event, no mediator shall willingly testify about any knowledge or communication received, and said mediator shall employ all legal efforts to resist the revelation of any information (California Evidence Code number 703.5 and 1152.5).

In some circumstances, individuals will feel much more comfortable knowing that fact (e.g., in cases of custody agreements, estate planning, etc.). At the end of this chapter, we provide you with some examples of forms that institutions have used to assure both voluntary participation and confidentiality in mediation sessions.

WHAT TO EXPECT:
THE PROCESS OF MEDIATION

After assuring that everyone is voluntarily participating, and that everyone will hold communication in the mediation session confidential, you will want to go over the process of mediation and the ground rules that everyone will need to follow in order to make the mediation process successful. Table 6.1 shows an overview of the process that we will detail in this section.

Initially, parties should understand that they will be asked to give an account of what has brought them to the mediation and perhaps talk about their goals for the process. In most cases, mediators will first ask each of the parties to talk to them as they give their account, and they will ask the other party to wait patiently during that time, after which they will be able to give their account to the mediators. In the next few chapters, we will discuss how mediators employ a variety of tools during this time that enable them to help the parties listen to, and better understand, each other. At first, many participants feel more comfortable addressing their concerns to the mediators than they do to the other party, and this helps create a safe environment for everyone to observe the expert modeling of effective communication provided by the mediator.

Next, in many cases, if participants are ready and they agree to it, mediators will encourage participants to talk directly to each other about their interests and concerns by following specific directions about their communication. In this case, mediators will monitor the communication closely to assure that participants are practicing active listening with each other and that they are following the ground rules for communication. Some mediators have specific "tricks of the trade" in which they have participants do certain communication exercises to open up communication. In the following chapters, we will highlight some of those exercises so that you can decide if you would like to include them in your own toolbox.

Hopefully, at some point, it will be clear to the mediator(s) that the participants are coming to an understanding about each other's interests and concerns. At this point, the mediator will suggest that participants engage in a brainstorming activity to think of ways in which they might resolve their dispute. Once options have been generated and exhausted, parties will be encouraged to deliberate about the options and try to come to agreement about specific ideas. Once parties have come to an initial agreement about a solution, the mediator will help them do a "reality check" in which they work on brainstorming what might go wrong with the solution, whether the solution really covers all of the areas of concern that were raised, and whether the solution is a realistic one for all parties. Finally, if everyone agrees and the reality check passes, the mediator(s) will help the parties write up the official agreement and the parties will sign the agreement to indicate their promise to follow it. The agreement remains a confidential document for the mediators and the parties; only if all parties agree can the agreement be shared outside the mediation session.

Caucusing

Sometimes during a mediation session, the process needs to be paused for a while. We discussed in Chapter 4 some of the reasons why mediators might choose to pause or stop the mediation process. One of the ways they might do this is to have a caucus.

A caucus might happen for two main reasons. One, if more than one mediator is used, the mediators may feel they need to talk privately about the process and how it is progressing. In this case, mediators might ask parties to take a short break (usually in separate rooms) during which the mediators discuss the mediation process.

The second reason mediators might call a caucus is to check in with parties individually to see how they are doing with the mediation process. In some cases, there may be some interpersonal dynamic affecting communication in the mediation session that can be worked out through a caucus. For instance, if it seems like one person is dominating the discussion, it might be a good idea to check in with both parties separately to make sure that everyone is comfortable with the process. In cases where there are power differences (parent-child, cultural clashes, etc.), a caucus can be used to help the person who is feeling less power to have a chance to speak and be heard. In all cases, it is important to make sure that when mediators are meeting separately with parties, that they do so in a equitable manner (i.e., not spending a lot of time with one party and only a minute or two with the other).

In the introduction, it is not necessary to give all of the details about a caucus, but it is ideal for participants to know about the possibility of a caucus. In some cases, individual parties may request a caucus because they would like to have a private conversation. Caucuses are always held in confidence.

Going Forward

Finally, after a discussion of the process of mediation, it is important to make sure that all of the participants feel comfortable with going forward. Asking them directly if they are okay with the process of the mediation is one way to ensure that the participants have bought into the process and that they will stay throughout its conclusion. Some mediators ask that the participants sign a form that is an "agreement to mediate," which says that the participants are informed about the process and are comfortable continuing with it.

At this point, participants may have some questions about the process. It is important for the mediators to address those questions with as much information as they can without getting into specifics about the conflict. It is also important that mediators trust in the process and ask that participants trust in the process as well; for instance, some participants may want to go straight to the brainstorming stage, but a mediator can assure them that first talking about their interests and concerns will make the brainstorming stage more effective in the long run.

Exercise: Creating Your Opening Cheat Sheet

Take a moment to write some notes about what you would like to say in your introduction to a mediation session. This could be in the form of an outline, some key phrases that you would like to remember, or a list of topics. Once you have a draft of your "cheat sheet," practice giving your introduction (often called an opening statement) to a fellow classmate or trainee.

1. What was the most comfortable part about giving the opening statement for you?
2. What felt most awkward as you were giving your introduction?
3. Were there any parts of the introduction that you left out in your practice?

As you work through these questions, go ahead and revise your introduction/opening statement cheat sheet so that you can have the notes in exactly the way you need them for a mediation session.

Table 6.1: Overview of the Mediation Process

Pre-Mediation
Case Development

*Send out confidentiality
and agreement to mediate forms*

Introduction Stage
Introduce mediators and parties

Words of encouragement
Explain process, definition of mediation and mediator roles
Ground rules
Confidentiality
Caucus possibility
Sign agreement to mediate
Ask for questions

Sharing Perspectives Stage

Listening to parties' positions	*Weed out interests, feelings and needs*
Parties actively listening to each other	*Restating*
Summarizing	*Asking questions*
Reframing	*Reflecting*
Acknowledging	*Validating*
Focusing on "I" instead of "you"	*Caucusing*

Understanding

Problem Solving Stage

Interests, not positions	*Objective criteria*
Issue framing	*Agenda setting*
Option generation	*Deliberating*

Resolution
Developing the agreement
Signing agreement form

7

Sharing Perspectives, Competence, and Attributions

In this chapter, we introduce the concept of sharing perspectives. We explain the reasons behind having parties share their perspectives and the different ways that mediators help parties through this process. Further, we will introduce theories associated with communication competence and attributions and discuss how those theories can help us understand how participants share perspectives in the mediation. Then, we will work through one or two cases that explore issues of power, communication competence, and attributions and discuss tactics for dealing with those issues as mediators.

SHARING PERSPECTIVES

Once the mediators and parties have finished their introductions and made clear that they would like to move forward with the mediation, it is time to start getting the parties to share their perspectives with the mediators and with each other. During this stage of the mediation, mediators work with parties to help them construct their perspectives in such a way that 1) the other party(ies) can listen to and hear them; 2) they focus on their own interests and not on positions; and 3) they are able to flesh out all of their concerns and needs. Mediators often take a two-step approach to sharing perspectives, but of course, like the rest of the mediation process, these two steps are fluid and flexible. You may start with one, move to the other, move back and forth, or use only one of the steps without the other. We will give you a typical scenario about how this might work, and you can practice and experiment until you find what works for you and the parties.

In the first step of sharing perspectives, many mediators ask the parties—one party at a time—to give their perspective to the mediator(s). Mediators who do this (ask parties to speak only to them at first) are striving to control the environment so that they can make sure there is a safe space for everyone to speak. Thus, as the parties share their perspectives with the mediator, the mediator models active listening and reframes any statements that seem incendiary. This gives both parties the opportunity to observe the mediator's communication style. The mediator also practices and demonstrates neutrality during this step by making sure that both parties have ample and equal speaking time. The parties can voice as many concerns as they can think of while doing so in a productive and interest-oriented way.

After talking with the parties for as much time as they think they need, mediators will want to have the parties start talking with each other. In this second step of sharing perspectives, mediators will ask parties to share with each other some of their main concerns while modeling the communication practices they have been working on with the mediator. At first, the mediator may direct this conversation by asking each party to share a particular concern and having the other party demonstrate active listening. However, parties often learn quickly; they may begin moving on in this step without prompting from the mediator. When that happens, the mediator can usually sit back and listen carefully to make sure that the parties continue to keep up their civil discourse.

Depending on the nature of the dispute, and the personalities of the parties involved, mediators might find themselves working in one of these steps longer than another, moving back and forth between them, or skipping one of them entirely. When we have had particularly difficult times getting our parties to talk to each other civilly, we have also *combined* these steps. In these cases, mediators must be extremely direct in their communication, and might ask party one to share a concern and then specifically ask party two to acknowledge that concern before moving on. In that way, the parties talk to each other *through* the mediator.

Sharing perspectives is often the most challenging and the most valuable part of the mediation process. Mediators will strive to make sure that parties feel heard, and that they hear each other. Thus, the parties will begin to model truly effective and appropriate communication with each other. This can be an empowering experience for both mediators and parties. In the next few sections, and in the next chapter, we will explore some theories behind the process of sharing perspectives that should help you to understand *why* these communication skills work and *how* they work. Our hope is that as you work through these theoretical explanations, you will begin to have a richer and fuller understanding of the "model" communicator you will become as a mediator.

COMMUNICATION COMPETENCE

Learning to communicate competently is a skill that individuals should continually practice. *Communication competence* occurs when we communicate in both an *effective* and *socially appropriate* manner. Our competence in many cases depends upon the social situation in which we find ourselves (Wilson & Sabee, 2003). Consider circumstances in which you feel that you communicate well and those in which you feel you do not communicate well. Make a list of the environments that you feel comfortable with and those that you do not. Consider the following example of such a list:

Good Communicator	Need Improvement
With friends	With supervisor
With brothers and sisters	With parents
One on one	Giving a speech

Of course, everyone's list will be different, but the idea is to start to understand when you believe you are both effective and socially appropriate at the same time. Sometimes it can be difficult to communicate in a socially appropriate manner if we do not know the cultural rules that are expected. For instance, in some circumstances and cultures individuals are encouraged to speak their mind publicly. In other cultures or circumstances, open criticism is not acceptable. It might be appropriate to use a different language with certain groups of people than with others. For example, some people use slang or cursing with their friends but not with their family or co-workers. Others may switch back and forth between languages (e.g., Spanish and English), depending on the circumstance or the person with whom they are communicating.

In many cases, people may find that they are not being heard in a conflict because they are either not communicating effectively or in a socially appropriate manner. It can be frustrating to try repeatedly to get your point across to others and find that they are *just not getting it*. For example, a couple of roommates who consulted one of us were having a problem communicating with each other. Both were frustrated because they felt like they were trying to be as clear as they possibly could with each other; however, each felt that the other was not hearing them. One of the roommates, Drew, was becoming more and more agitated by the fact that the other was not picking up their things from the dining room table. Since they both used the dining room table to do work from home, Drew found it important that the table be clear when he wanted to use it; otherwise; he would have to clear it off and that just added more work for him. Drew felt that his roommate, Nita, should clear her things when she was not using the table.

In order to communicate to Nita that she should clear the table when she was not using it, Drew would pile all of her things into a laundry basket and put it on her bed. He did not want to nag her about it because he felt that was not polite, and he didn't want to have a confrontation. Since he was doing this every day, he thought that Nita would get the hint that he wanted her to clear the table. However, Nita was becoming agitated that Drew was throwing all of her organized things into a basket and putting them on her bed. She thought that he was being rude since she had left them on the table in a specific order so that she could return to work with them later. However, because she did not want a confrontation, she stopped talking to Drew unless she had to. She thought that this "silent treatment" would make it clear that she was upset about his behavior and that he would stop it.

By the time Nita approached one of us, she was upset enough that she wanted to move out of her apartment and into a different living situation. However, since she and Drew had signed a lease together, they needed to work with a mediator to discover how they would work out the rent/subleasing issues for the remainder of the lease. When they began to talk through their concerns and interests in the mediation session, they realized that they could have resolved this dispute much earlier. Both felt badly about their misunderstandings, and they were able to work out an agreement in which they remained roommates, with both having their own space to use however they wanted for their work.

A major problem with Nita and Drew's communication was that they were not being *effective*. Both of them felt that it was not appropriate or desirable to have a "confrontation" with the other about their concerns. Therefore, they used a "hinting" strategy for communicating with each other. This kind of communication strategy is quite *indirect* and *polite*, but it is often unclear, requiring some "translation" (Brown & Levinson, 1987). People in conflict need to understand how the other person is understanding their communication. In many cases, they will find that more direct communication can help them better understand how they are being perceived.

Within a mediation session, the mediator will help coach the participants with more effective and socially appropriate communication. For instance, mediators will ask direct questions about the interests and concerns of the parties. In many cases, no one has ever directly asked the participants these questions before, and they had no reason to articulate the answers. For instance, Drew had never asked Nita why she was upset with him; he just thought she was being rude (leaving her stuff on the table) and cold (not talking to him). He felt alienated and intimidated about talking to her and thus, she had no opportunity to share her feelings with him. During the mediation, however, we were able to ask her directly about her concerns and feelings, and Drew was able to hear them for the first time. Likewise, Nita was able to hear Drew's concerns for the first time.

Mediators will also help coach parties on socially appropriate communication practices. For instance, when participants are in conflict, the high emotions often result in people blaming each other or becoming defensive with each other. This is socially inappropriate because people generally do not like someone telling them that they are at fault for some transgression—it is considered impolite. However, when mediators proactively *reframe* inappropriate communication, the parties find that they are more willing to listen to each other. Mediators help participants to communicate more appropriately; people are generally more willing and able to listen to socially appropriate communication than to inappropriate communication.

When people from different cultures find themselves in conflict, socially appropriate communication is not always clear to both parties. In a recent mediation involving a neighbor dispute, one of us encountered two neighbors who were having difficulty coming to a resolution over a barking dog (case 4.2). For Jim and Melissa, the couple with the dog, their dog was like their child. They treated it well, trained it, and spoke to it in a moderate tone. However, their neighbor, Vui, was an older woman who had emigrated to the United States many years ago from Vietnam. She was frightened by the dog when it would bark and she responded by yelling at the dog. She felt that, as an older woman who worked hard (over sixty hours a week), she should not be bothered by the dog barking when she went out to enjoy her backyard. She often cooked her meals in the backyard and felt that, even though there was a fence, the barking of the dog intruded on her serene surroundings. Her neighbors were upset that she would yell at their dog so loudly, and she was upset that her neighbors would not respect her age and her environment. However, by the time they began talking to each other about what to do, they were already at odds regarding their *positions* instead of their *interests*.

Jim and Melissa wanted their neighbor to stop yelling at their dog (which they thought was reasonable because the dog responded better to gentler handling). Vui wanted her neighbors to keep the dog inside when she was at home (since she worked so much she was not often at home and felt it was a reasonable request). However, both parties were angry with each other and could not see the common ground that lay between their positions. Neither wanted to "give in" to the other's requests, because both felt that they had been disrespected.

Through the mediation, we discovered that Vui actually felt uncomfortable in her neighborhood because many of the neighbors did not treat her as she expected to be treated given her age. In her home country, people would have been more open and helpful with older citizens. She felt like an outsider and thought she had to defend herself in every disagreement. Her defensive attitude led the other neighbors to think she was rude and did not want to interact with them. Thus, even though Vui longed for a sense of community, the other neighbors interpreted her communication as if she wanted to be left alone.

While we were not able to reach an agreement in that mediation, both parties were able to understand each other better. They left the mediation agreeing to talk with each other more, and Jim and Melissa worked to help the other neighbors understand Vui's needs. When we called to check in on the parties after six weeks, we found that they had reached an agreement on their own with which everyone was happy. Even though the mediation itself did not end in an official agreement, the parties learned enough about each other during their session to resolve their conflicts more productively and to communicate with each other in a more appropriate manner. Just learning about each other's cultures helped them to work out their issues. Moreover, since people generally will comply with agreements better when they come up with them themselves, we were quite happy to find that they did this without our assistance.

Attribution Theory

Attribution theory suggests that people have specific perceptions about events for which they make causal attributions. Better understanding of the perceptions people have about those with whom they have conflict is through attributions. *Attributions* are causal inferences about the reasons that events occur. Weiner's (1986) attribution theory of motivation and emotion suggests that the attributions individuals make for an event are related to their emotions and behavior. Specifically, Weiner suggested that when people encounter an event, their emotions and their understanding of the cause of the event lead them to make causal attributions about it.

Weiner (1986) suggested three dimensions of attributions that can be made for a causal event: locus (or location), stability, and controllability. The locus dimension refers to *where* the cause for the event is located; or, more generally, whether a cause for an event can be attributed to internal (caused by the attributor) or external (caused by some outside factor) forces. It is common for individuals to foster a *self-serving bias* when deciding whether attributions are internal or external. For instance, we often assume it is not our fault when an undesirable event occurs, (i.e., it was due to some external factor); whereas, when a desirable event occurs, we tend to assume that it was our doing (i.e., it was due to some internal factor). In conflicts, we may end up assuming that someone is "at fault" for an undesirable event, even if the other person would perceive the event to be caused by external factors.

The stability dimension refers to the variability of the cause—specifically, whether the cause changes over time. In some cases, individuals may perceive that the cause for an event will continue to be stable and thus become frustrated about it. For instance, when working with a customer service representative, some people may feel that their needs are not being met and that the customer service rep is not hearing them. They may assume that the cause for this lies within the system of the customer service department (i.e., a stable cause) rather than in a single bad experience (i.e., an unstable cause).

The controllability dimension refers to whether someone, or some organization, has control over a cause. The *fundamental attribution error* suggests that people generally assume that the cause of an upsetting event is *intentional*. For example, if we are driving on the freeway and another person cuts us off, a common fundamental attribution would be to think that the driver cut us off because he is a rude or selfish person, and is in control of the situation. However, in most cases, people cut others off because they do not see them, or they need to change lanes in a hurry to avoid some danger in the road.

The attributions that people make for an event are directly related to the emotions they feel about it, which may drive their consequent behavior. For example, a student who earns a low evaluation on an assignment may attribute the low evaluation to a lack of effective studying (internal attribution) or to an instructor's lack of clarity explaining the assignment (external attribution). The student making an internal attribution may study more in the future to receive a higher evaluation in the future. A student making an external attribution may not study more; instead, the student may attempt to communicate with the instructor about grading standards (Sabee & Wilson, 2005). Or if the student feels that the instructor will not clarify the requirements, the student may give up on doing better in the future—a form of learned helplessness (e.g., Dweck, 2000; Lefcourt, 1976). Indeed, scholars have demonstrated links between the attributions that individuals make for an event and the communication behavior that they engage in surrounding that event (e.g., MacGeorge, 2001; Sabee & Wilson, 2005).

Although substantial research has suggested that the locus of attributions individuals make may affect their future behavior (Dweck, 2000; Lefcourt, 1976; Rotter, 1954; Weiner, 1986), individuals also may interact with others differently because they make attributions that substantially affect their relationships (Curtis, 1994; Sabee et al., 2007). For instance, Curtis (1994) looked into the attributions that physical therapists made about their conversations with physicians. Physical therapists were asked to describe a conversation in which they felt successful with a physician and then one in which they felt unsuccessful. Those who initially had the lowest expectations for future compromise of their judgment (i.e., they thought they were right and could convince the physician) attributed their outcomes following failure to internal causes. Whereas, those who had high expectations of future compromise of their judgment (i.e., they did not feel they would be able to convince the physician) tended to attribute failure to external causes. In other words, if physical therapists expected a physician to ask them to do something that they did not agree with, they assumed that their failure to convince the physician was because of an external cause. However, if they believed that the physician would not ask them to do something that they did not agree with, they assumed that their failure to convince the physician was because of an internal cause. This finding suggests that individuals' attributions for behavior are related to past experiences and established relationships.

Causal attributions are related to communication behavior. Research suggests that the types of attributions individuals make for an event are associated with their interaction goals (e.g., MacGeorge, 2001; Sabee & Wilson, 2005), compliance seeking behaviors they employ (e.g., Wilson, Cruz, Marshall, & Rao, 1993), their relational qualities (e.g., Curtis, 1994; Sabee et al., 2007), and their marital satisfaction (e.g., Bradbury & Fincham, 1990). MacGeorge (2001) found that attributions made by a support-provider about a support-seeker's situation influenced the communication goals the provider had for the interaction and the ways that the support-provider communicated support messages. Sabee and Wilson (2005) found that the attributions students made about the receipt of a negative grade influenced the goals they had for an interaction about that negative grade with their instructor. Research on marital interaction has suggested that when one spouse makes attributions for the negative behavior of the other spouse, this influences the satisfaction that individuals have in their marital relationship (for a review, see Bradbury & Fincham, 1990).

Bippus (2003) investigated the attributions made concerning the reasons that individuals used humor in recalled conflict episodes. She found that internal attributions about the reasons that a conflict partner used humor (e.g., decreasing one's anxiety) were associated with negative feelings; whereas, external attributions about those reasons (e.g., making the other person feel better) were associated with positive feelings. This means that when we make attributions about events, or the ways that others communicate, it affects our perspective of the conversations we have with them as well as the ways we choose to communicate.

Mediators need to pay careful attention to the attributions that individuals have about the events surrounding their conflicts. Asking questions that clarify the kinds of attributions the parties are making will help mediators understand how each party perceives the event surrounding the conflict. It will also help each party hear how the other perceives the event. Imagine if you were able to talk to the person that cut you off on the freeway. You might learn that they saw a hubcap fall from the car in front of them and needed to get out of the way quickly. You would probably feel much less frustration, knowing that they were just trying to avoid an accident, than if you simply assumed they were not paying attention on the road.

CONCLUSION

The way we communicate with each other is important to our relationships—especially so when we are in conflict. Making sure that people communicate competently, in both an effective and socially appropriate manner, and that they begin to understand the attributions they make surrounding events, is a skill that mediators can use to help people communicate with each other when they share their perspectives in a mediation. Please take some time to work through the case studies following this chapter to understand more about how a mediator can help parties learn about each other and, hopefully, come to resolution based on that knowledge.

CASE 7.1
ROAD RAGE

The background of this victim-offender mediation session was that a boy of about thirteen was nearly run over by a car as he rode his bike to school. Someone saw the accident and got the license plate of the car that nearly ran him down. The driver was arrested, and the case came to the mediation program from the district attorney's office. The boy lived with his grandparents as his parents were unfit to care for him.

At the mediation session, the grandparents were furious with the offender and wanted him sent back to Vietnam (he was a legal immigrant in the United States). They accused him of almost killing their grandson who had already suffered enough because of the separation from his parents; to have this happen to him was more than they could handle. In this mediation, the grandparents needed the driver to hear how frightened and upset they were.

The Vietnamese man who had almost run over the boy was so scared he was shaking, and the mediators had to have a translator interpret for him. He shared with the grandparents that the morning of the incident, he got a call from his son's school saying that they were worried that his son might have been kidnapped. They wanted him to come to the school as soon as possible. Because he had been so focused on his own troubles, he was unaware of the boy on the bicycle. He did not realize that the boy had been in any danger until he was arrested.

After sharing their perspectives with the mediators, both sides were able to calm down enough to talk with each other as the mediators coached them. Once all parties had been heard, the grandparents decided to drop the charges. The grandmother felt that a huge burden had been lifted from her shoulders upon learning that the man had not intentionally hit her grandson's bike and that the man was in such a hurry because he was terrified that his son had been kidnapped from school. The Vietnamese man said how sorry he was and was extremely relieved that the charges were dropped.

1. What attributions were the parties making about the cause of these events?

    _____

    _____

    _____

    _____

2. Do you think that the resolution was a fair one? Why or why not?

    _____

    _____

    _____

    _____

3. How do you think that cultural or social backgrounds influenced this dispute and/or the mediation?

    _____

    _____

    _____

    _____

CASE 7.2
HIGH SCHOOL GANGS

A local high school called the county mediation program and asked some mediators to come to the school to settle a problem between two gangs—an Asian gang and an African American gang. The mediators first met with the six African American students. They were upset at how the school was treating them. As they voiced their concerns, they were highly agitated, but once they all had a chance to say their piece, it became clear that they were concerned that the school was listening to the other minorities and not paying attention to them. They felt that they were being targeted for discipline and left out of decision-making.

The mediators then met with the eight Asian students. Interestingly, they shared that they had no dispute with the African American students. The mediators were amazed by the incorrect assumptions that they had made throughout the case development. Because the school administration had called them, they trusted that the school administration had already completed the case development. When the mediators brought the two student groups together, the Asian students explained that they had no issues with the African American students.

As it turned out, the dispute was between the African American students and the administrators at the high school. The mediators set up a meeting with the African American students and the high school staff. Because the mediators had spent time previously working with the students on their communication, they were able to share that the students felt left out of the school activities and felt they were unjustly blamed for many things that had happened at the school. The parties worked out an agreement stating that the school would plan certain events for school activities that the African American group initiated; they would also provide opportunities to insure that they felt included in all activities. The administration also agreed to invite the group into the principal's office for a conversation before being accused of any activity that was against the school rules. The bottom line was that other minorities had come into the school, displacing the African American group as the center of attention. The school was relieved that it was not a gang problem but rather two benign groups of students.

1. What went wrong in the case development for this mediation? What assumptions were made about the dispute and the parties? Which of those assumptions turned out to be accurate and which were not?

   _____

   _____

   _____

   _____

2. Were the parties communicating in effective and appropriate ways before the mediation? What were they doing that was competent? What was incompetent?

   _____

   _____

   _____

   _____

3. What attributions do you think that the students and the administration were making? Were any of these attributions reframed to help reach a resolution?

   _____

   _____

   _____

   _____

CASE 7.3
FAMILY FEUDS

A family-friendly apartment complex is enclosed with fences and gates for the protection of the residents, especially the children. The established practice among parents is to watch each other's children when they are in the courtyard. When a new family moves in from Taiwan, they are happy to see such a cooperative environment; they see it as mirroring some of their own practices in their home country around collective involvement among families.

One day a police officer knocks on the door of the Taiwanese family's apartment and tells them that they received a call from neighbors about a child wandering on the street. When they arrived, they found the family's three-year-old walking in the road that surrounds the complex. They cited the parents for child endangerment, and the parents were given a court date to explain their behavior and to prove to the court that they could provide for the safety of their children. Failure to do so could mean that child protective services would be given jurisdiction for the safety of the children. The Taiwanese family not only was baffled that no one in the courtyard was watching their child and allowed the child to get outside the gate, but also that their neighbors would call the police and not come directly to them with any concern they had about child safety.

The neighbor who called the police saw the situation quite differently. She was concerned that the Taiwanese family seemed to take advantage of any parent who was in the courtyard and sent their children out to play whenever they perceived there was an opportunity to get rid of their children for an extended period. While the courtyard practice is that a parent who is outside with their own child will ordinarily watch another family's child, it is assumed that the parents will ask each other first. The other typically understood courtyard practice is that parents also watch their child from their apartment. This neighbor had seen the Taiwanese parents send their kids outside and lock the door to the apartment so the children could not get back in. It was reported that the child who was picked up by the police had been crying outside their apartment door, asking to get in for a long time before he was finally attended to by his parents. The neighbor had talked to the family about leaving their children outside, felt that previous conversations had not stopped the parents' practice, and wanted authorities to determine what should be done to protect the children.

The Taiwanese family thought they were conforming to a Western practice that was close to their own cultural experience. They were frightened by the intervention of the police and worried that they would lose their children because the state would find them unfit. Reporting someone to officials in their old country was very intimidating. They were angry with their neighbors. The neighbors felt that attempts to change the parents' behavior through reminders had failed. They were concerned about the children's welfare and wanted to avoid a face-to-face argument with the parents.

1. Awareness of, and sensitivity to, local and international customs can become critical in relationship building and maintenance. What assumptions did these parties make about each other's behavior, and how did those assumptions add to their dispute? What assumptions do you make? Do you think that one party is more "right" than another is in this situation?

   _____

   _____

   _____

   _____

2. Beliefs about the sanctity of parental primacy in dealing with issues involving ones children, versus having other authorities involved, is a sensitive issue with regard to international members of communities—whether they are immigrants or permanent residents. How did the assumptions of parental primacy influence the attributions that each party made about the other?

   _____

   _____

   _____

   _____

3. What attention to cultural practice would you take as a mediator to make sure that communication was both effective and socially appropriate in this situation? How could you work to bring the parties toward understanding about such an important issue?

   _____

   _____

   _____

   _____

8

Sharing Perspectives, Goals, and Face

In this chapter, we continue our discussion of sharing perspectives, and focus the discussion on interaction goals and face management. Specifically, we will consider how interaction goals can affect parties in the mediation process and how we can work to change problematic interaction goals. Further, we will discuss face management as an important consideration for parties, and look at how culture and difference can affect how face is managed and affected by the process.

INTERACTION GOALS AND SHARING PERSPECTIVES

Communication is a strategic process in that individuals usually have goals that they wish to attain while communicating. The goals that people have are not always conscious goals, but we tend to have goals at many different degrees of consciousness while we are communicating. Sometimes, when we want to do something like purchase an automobile for a good price, we have very conscious and discrete goals. Other times, our goals are less discrete—like maintaining a relationship while having a difficult discussion.

Interaction goals fall into two distinct categories. First, individuals have a primary goal at a given point in a conversation. The primary goal drives the conversation and acts as a sort of "push" force wherein individuals strive to use communication to achieve their goal. To figure out what a primary goal is at a specific point during a conversation, imagine that you could hit a "pause" button and ask one of the communicators what they are *doing* at that moment in their conversation and you would identify the primary goal. Examples of primary goals may be to *ask a favor from a friend* (Wilson, Aleman & Leatham, 1998), *comfort someone* on the loss of a loved one (MacGeorge, 2001), or attempt to *change a disappointing evaluation* in a conversation with a superior or a teacher (Sabee & Wilson, 2005). Second, individuals have secondary goals that constrain their interaction and act as a "pull" force. These goals are many times in contrast to the primary goal and they help to shape the way in which people strive to achieve their primary goal. Examples of secondary goals may include maintaining a relationship (Dillard, Segrin & Hardin, 1999), not appearing "nosy" (Wilson, Aleman & Leatham, 1998), or maintaining a boundary of privacy (Sabee, 2007).

Primary and secondary goals work together in that a primary goal drives the interaction—pushing the accelerator—and the secondary goals pull back on the interaction—pressing a bit on the brakes. That way, even though you might want your friend to loan you fifty dollars (your primary goal), you might approach the friend by assuring that that you will pay back the money right away (attending to your identity goals), and that you will understand if your friend cannot afford it right now (attending to your relationship goals). It is unlikely that you would simply say, "Hey Chris—loan me fifty bucks."

Table 8.1: Examples of Primary and Secondary Goals

Primary Goals (pushing the interaction)	Secondary Goals (pulling the interaction)
Ask a favor	Don't appear pushy
Comfort a friend	Respect their unique situation
Give some advice	Don't appear nosy
Learn more about course material	Appear as a competent student Don't infringe too much on teacher's time
Ask friend to pay back owed money	Don't appear as a push-over Don't appear pushy

The goals that we have in conversations often change throughout our interactions. In any given conversation, people have multiple primary and secondary goals, which are influenced by the interaction itself. For instance, a conversation may start with one person having a primary goal of asking a favor of a friend. This person probably also has some secondary goals, including not appearing pushy, maintaining established boundaries in their relationship and making sure that they appear competent in their interaction. However, upon finding out that the friend will not be able to do the favor because of the loss of a beloved pet, their primary goal may quickly change to that of comforting their friend, while having secondary goals of not appearing nosy, and of being seen as an understanding and caring individual. In most conversations, goals will change multiple times, and sometimes goals that began as secondary goals will move into a primary goal position.

Our goals are affected by the appraisals and attributions that we make; and if we change appraisals or attributions, we may likely change our goals as well. Remember, attributions are accounts that we make for causal events—the reasons we think that events occur. Our "appraisals" of those events occur in tandem with our attributions. In other words, we enter into an event, make an appraisal about what is going on, make attributions about what has happened, and then make decisions about what we will say in an interaction. Imagine that you have scheduled a meeting with two of your fellow classmates or co-workers because you are all working on a project together. You arrive at your agreed upon location on time, and find that they are not there. You wait for about twenty minutes before they finally show up, laughing and talking as they enter the room. How would you appraise this situation (what do you think is going on)? What attributions are you likely to make about their tardiness?

You may be upset that your colleagues arrived late to the meeting and appear jovial (rather than apologetic) about their lateness. You may start with a primary goal of getting to work on your project right away (because of all that wasted time). You may also have some secondary goals of demonstrating that you do not appreciate them taking advantage of your time (an identity goal), and you still want to do a good job on this project together (a relational goal). The attributions that you made (it must be their fault for being late and they do not seem to care) could color how you approach this interaction. However, if you refrain from addressing their lateness, you may not find out from your colleagues that they were late because one of them had just found out that she had been denied a promotion she was really looking forward to and had expected. The other colleague, finding the first in a very emotional state, tried to make her feel better by distracting her with funny stories. Because the person who failed to get the promotion was very upset, it had taken the other colleague a while to get her calmed down and ready to go to your meeting.

Now, you may still be upset about the loss of your own time, but also you may change your attributions a little. You might think that your colleagues have more acceptable (and more external) reasons for behaving as they did, and you might now approach your interaction differently than you would have before changing your attributions. Therefore, you may realize that your interaction goals should be different than they once were. You may change your primary goal to helping comfort your colleague, seeing if your partners would like to schedule a better time to work since they might not feel up to it just now, or discussing a more appropriate division of labor than the one that you had originally agreed upon.

When mediators understand the different types of interaction goals that people have, they may be able to help them address those interaction goals more specifically. Primary and secondary interaction goals will shape the communication in a mediation; it is important for mediators to recognize goals for all parties, especially when they are conflicting goals. For instance, if both parties have secondary goals that they would like to appear the "winner" of this dispute, then the mediators have more to work through than just the issues surrounding the dispute. They need to address those secondary goals either explicitly, or through careful management of the communication in the mediation session.

Our goals may change throughout a conversation for many reasons. Secondary goals will shape the nature of how people try to pursue primary interaction goals. For instance, people often think that it is important to portray a positive image during an interaction (identity goal). Depending on who you are and what kind of "self" you want to portray, you may find that your "identity goals" are different than another's. For instance, one person may not want to appear to be a "push over" by "giving in" to demands of the other party. This secondary goal can impede the primary goal of "settling the dispute." Whether or not people feel comfortable with a suggested resolution, they may not want to agree to it if they believe that agreeing will make it seem like other people could get whatever they wanted in the future. Their identity goal might constrain their interaction so much that they do not accomplish their primary goal.

A mediator who recognizes that one party is being constrained by such a powerful secondary goal can help to smooth the interaction by specifically addressing that secondary goal. In some cases, it may be appropriate to have a caucus to discuss the party's needs and feelings. One party may feel intimidated by the other party, or impeded from working through other issues, depending on how this issue/dispute is settled. Perhaps having a chance to talk through those things in an environment without the other party would help that person to reprioritize his goals. On the other hand, sometimes it may be important to talk through these issues with all parties present. If the constrained party feels less intimidated but still impeded (i.e., giving in this time may set an unwanted precedent), then it may be important for the other party to hear that so that it is addressed in the agreement.

CASE 8.1
NOISY NEIGHBORS AND UNDERLYING INTERACTIONS

A neighborhood mediation program received a call from a couple who had been having difficulty with their neighbor. They had moved into their apartment a couple of months earlier, and the downstairs neighbor had complained about how noisy they were. The couple who called could not understand their downstairs neighbors' complaints; they felt they were relatively quiet people and they took care to keep the volume down on their television and radio. When they received the first complaint, they talked with their neighbors and thought they had come to an understanding. However, since then, the downstairs neighbors had been leaving notes on their doorstep stating their complaints.

The couple called the mediation program because they hoped that mediators could help them work out this issue. They planned on living in the apartment for at least another two years and did not want strained relations with their neighbors. The mediation program set up a meeting and all of the neighbors met to discuss their concerns.

During the initial stage of perspective sharing, the mediators listened as the upstairs neighbors, Ariel and Darrin, discussed their perspective. They felt like they had been reasonably quiet neighbors, and they were concerned and feeling harassed by the notes left by their downstairs neighbors. When the downstairs neighbors, Daniela and Korin, shared their concerns, they noted that they had a discussion with the upstairs neighbors about the noise, but that they were disappointed when nothing seemed to change. Thinking that the upstairs neighbors were ignoring them, they became frustrated with the situation.

Both sets of neighbors continued to share their concerns. It seemed as if they both wanted to work with each other, but they were having difficulty coming up with any acceptable ideas for a solution to their problems. While the mediators felt that they had made good progress with getting the neighbors to understand each other, they found themselves at a standstill when it came to working through solutions. So they decided to caucus. They talked first with Daniela and Korin. When they asked them why they thought it was so difficult for the group to come up with solutions, they learned some important information. While Daniela and Korin did not have a problem working with Ariel and Darrin, they were frustrated by outside factors, which they felt were disrupting their ability to come to a solution.

They shared that they had been having some difficulties with their landlord. They had made several complaints about how thin the walls and ceilings were and had asked for more insulation, but the landlord had not complied. They also shared that when the previous upstairs neighbors moved from their apartment, that Daniela and Korin had asked if they could move to that apartment so that the noise did not bother them as much. The landlord informed them that they could move only if they were willing to pay 15 percent more in their rent, which they were not prepared to do. However, they discovered through advertisements on the local bulletin board that the landlord was offering the upstairs apartment at the same rent that they were paying. They had confirmed this with Ariel and Darrin when they first moved in. Daniela and Korin were upset at how the landlord had treated them. They did not really want to resolve the dispute with their neighbors; what they really wanted was to make the landlord fix the insulation and admit that he had acted inappropriately by not allowing them to move.

This information was important to the mediators. Now, they understood that, while the two sets of neighbors both had the goal of getting along and being able to live with each other peacefully, Daniela and Korin were more concerned about making a point to their landlord than they were about maintaining a civil relationship with Ariel and Darrin. The mediators asked Daniela and Korin to share this information with their upstairs neighbors, and they did. The upstairs neighbors understood their concerns about the landlord and offered to try and help them by jointly writing a letter about the noise. However, it became clear during the discussion that this dispute would not be resolved unless Daniela and Korin would be able to work this out with the landlord. Thus, at the end of this mediation session, Daniela and Korin asked the mediation program to help them by inviting their landlord to a mediation so that they could work out their issues.

1. What primary goals did each set of neighbors have? What secondary goals did they have? Do you think that these goals changed during the mediation?

   _____

   _____

   _____

2. One of the reasons that Daniela and Korin thought the landlord was discriminating against them (not mentioned in the case study) is that they were in a same-sex romantic relationship. How do you think that this might have colored Daniela and Korin's secondary goals?

   _____

   _____

   _____

3. At the end of this mediation session, the dispute was not completely resolved. What goals do you think that each set of neighbors was able to achieve and what goals do you think they were unable to achieve?

FACE AND FACE MANAGEMENT

When Erving Goffman (1967) first described "face," he did so by going through a theatrical metaphor. He described the face that we wear in social interaction as our *performance* of our social image. Thus, when people engage in social interaction, in a way they are performing; they are projecting the image they want people to see. *Face*, or the positive social image that we would like to portray in social interaction, is an incredibly influential aspect of our identity and our communication, and it can be an important part of dispute resolution. Because it is such an important part of our identity, we must maintain "face" in our interactions in order to feel safe and comfortable.

Face, in fact, is so important to our social well-being that we tend to work cooperatively in social interaction to both maintain our own face *and* that of others (Brown & Levinson, 1987). *Politeness theory* suggests that we look out for each other's face during our interactions—thus, we typically will not do anything to *threaten* another's face without making some sort of *account* for it. For example, many people will refrain from giving criticism to others because they fear that it will hurt the other's feelings, or threaten their positive social image (face). However, when people do offer criticism, they often do so by accounting for the face threat. One common way to offer criticism is to first offer a compliment. For example, "You really do a nice job of organizing your thoughts in this email, but you might consider doing an extra spell check in the future because there are a few errors." In this criticism, we have given both a *compliment* and a *reason* (there are errors) for the criticism. These kinds of "politeness strategies" tend to soften the blow when we feel the need to threaten other people's face.

Our face is not one-sided; rather, it is a complex concept with many different aspects. While it would be impossible to cover all of those aspects in this text, we will focus on two major dimensions of face that we should consider when enacting polite communication strategies. Positive face is our desire for social affirmation. We maintain our positive face by making and keeping friends, enjoying affirmation through communication with others, and being approachable so that others like to spend time with us. Negative face, on the other hand, is our desire for personal autonomy. This is not negative as in "bad," but it is substantially different from positive face. In fact, rather than thinking about positive and negative as good and bad, use a "chemistry" metaphor to think about it. When scientists observe positively charged particles in an ion (protons), they see them being "attracted" to a nucleus. Whereas, they observe negatively charged particles (electrons) in an ion flying about in the nucleon shell, which is farther away from the nucleus. The positively charged particles strive for togetherness (they stick to the nucleus and do not move away); whereas the negatively charged particles strive for independence (they move freely around the atom). We maintain our negative face by asserting our independence, establishing boundaries, and being seen as people who can handle our own concerns.

Each person has different types of positive and negative face needs, and these needs not only work together, but also they are in tension with one another. We can be both autonomous and in control of our own lives *and* be well liked and receive positive affirmation. There may be specific times, however, when one of our face needs seems to be more important than another. Sometimes, when we have experienced a traumatic event, our needs for positive affirmation and comforting seem to outweigh our needs for control; thus, we may be more willing to let others "take care of us" in times of need because it is more important for us at that time to be comforted. To know what kinds of face needs exist, we need to be able to understand the context of a specific situation and specific individual.

Not only does the context of a situation affect the kinds of face needs we have, our context of culture also becomes important when considering face. Some groups of people consider certain face needs more important than others; it is important to be able to recognize when that is the case. Consider the following example:

Gabbi grew up in a very "independent" culture. The people with whom she interacted valued an individual's independence as a rite of passage into adulthood. Gabbi was very pleased that she was able to lead such an independent life; she took care of herself financially and she had a strong will. Being an independent and autonomous person was an important part of Gabbi's identity. In her social world, needing people to take care of you meant that something was wrong and you were somehow deficient. Of course, Gabbi valued helping people in need, but she did not want to be one of the people "in need."

When Gabbi began to befriend her neighbor, Trina, she was excited to find that Trina shared some of her interests in gardening and in sports. Both women began their friendship by talking about their common interests and learning from each other's experiences. However, as their relationship progressed, Gabbi started to be concerned about their friendship. One day after work, Gabbi came home to find that Trina had gone into Gabbi's garden to lay mulch. Gabbi had been planning to do that for a couple of weeks, but had not gotten around to it yet. When she asked Trina about it, Trina explained that she had procured the mulch from the city at no cost; since she had extra, she thought she would share. While Gabbi realized that this was a nice gesture, she had been looking forward to doing the mulching herself, and she felt weird about Trina doing it. Nevertheless, she did not feel that it would be polite to say anything about it.

However, Gabbi started to feel even more uncomfortable when similar things kept happening. She would arrive home from work and find that Trina had mowed her lawn (because she was mowing her own anyway and it seemed easy enough to do), or that Trina had given her some magazine articles about sports. While these all seemed like nice enough things for Trina to do, Gabbi could not shake the feeling that Trina was trying to "one-up" her. Every time she did something for Gabbi after that, Gabbi felt like it was a message that she was not doing things correctly (e.g., Gabbi didn't mow the lawn on time, Gabbi wasn't following the right biking trails, etc.). Finally, Gabbi no longer felt comfortable with their friendship, and she only talked to Trina when she really had to. In fact, she found herself avoiding Trina, which only made her angrier because she felt like she could not move freely about her own yard.

What went so terribly wrong with this friendship? As it turns out, Trina was making repeated face threats to Gabbi and not *accounting* for them. Every time she did something for Gabbi, Trina was, in a way, suggesting that Gabbi could not do it herself, which is a threat to negative face. For someone who comes from a very independent culture, these threats to negative face were insulting and resulted in Gabbi not wanting to continue the friendship.

Trina, however, did not understand that what she was doing was insulting. In fact, because Trina came from an interdependent culture, where people valued relationships and working together more than they valued independence, Trina felt that doing things for Gabbi was a way of strengthening their friendship. In Trina's culture, doing things for another person was a way of showing great respect for that person and of demonstrating that person's value. She could not understand why, when she would do such nice things for Gabbi, that Gabbi seemed to be upset about it. When she realized that Gabbi was pulling away from their friendship, Trina thought that she should do *more* nice things for her to make sure that Gabbi understood how much she was valued. However, when Gabbi continued to pull away, Trina felt badly about herself and about Gabbi—who she now thought of as a rude individual.

These misunderstandings were unfortunate, but they illustrate how a particular person's orientation toward their "face" can affect their relationships and communication. Trina and Gabbi had different face needs, but they failed to recognize those differences. While these two individuals would probably not come to a mediation session to patch their relationship and work on communication, they would find themselves in a situation in which they had difficulty managing a dispute and attend mediation for that reason. When a windstorm blew a tree from Gabbi's yard into Trina's, the two found themselves needing to work together. The tree had smashed the fence between the two women's yards. A large portion of the tree had fallen in Trina's yard. Gabbi suggested that she should clean up and pay for the tree damage in her yard and that Trina should clean up and pay for the damage in her yard. In Gabbi's mind, this lessened the amount of time the two women would have to spend together to solve this problem. However, because Trina felt that Gabbi had been rude and selfish to her in the past, she now felt that Gabbi was being selfish again. After all, it was Gabbi's tree; legally, she was responsible for any damage that it caused. In addition, the tree had ruined a prized vegetable garden in Trina's yard that she would have to replace. Trina felt that she was being stuck with the cost of fixing half of the fence, removing half of the tree, and replacing her garden, all because Gabbi had not removed a tree that was not sturdy enough to stand a windstorm.

So Trina suggested that Gabbi help her with the damage in her yard since it was so extensive. Gabbi did not want to, and then Trina said that Gabbi would have to take care of all of the damage, which was legally her responsibility. Gabbi was hurt that Trina would make that demand; plus, she was also unable to afford such extensive repairs. Thus, the women found themselves attending mediation to resolve their dispute. However, mediation could not succeed until the issues surrounding the past relationship were uncovered. Specifically, the mediators needed to uncover the different orientations to face that the two women had, and then help the women understand each other's different orientations. It would make a big difference to both women to understand why the other acted as she did in the past. Moreover, those past understandings would make it much easier for the women to come to an acceptable resolution and even to renew their friendship with better understanding of each other.

Face threats are common when parties are in conflict. There are several face threats that seem like obvious forms of communication, which mediators should watch for in a mediation session. These include insults, criticisms, reprimands or accusations (all threats to a person's positive face—or their desire for social affirmation), or orders, threats, warnings and dares (all threats to a person's negative face—or their desire for personal autonomy) (Brown & Levinson, 1987). As mediators, we should recognize that these kinds of statements need to be reframed. When mediators reframe these kinds of statements, they are many times using politeness strategies to neutralize the power of the face threat that has occurred.

However, other communication actions can also be threatening to a person's face that we do not automatically think of as problem statements. For instance, when people give suggestions, advice, or reminders about things, they may actually be suggesting that the other person do something that they might otherwise not choose to do, which is a threat to their personal autonomy. Even the most polite "suggestion" can be face threatening in certain environments. We especially find that in situations with parents and children in mediation sessions. The parents may offer advice and make suggestions; but when they do so, they threaten the negative face of their children and the dispute becomes more difficult to resolve. Further, it is important to recognize that mediators need to take the same careful concern. Mediators should refrain from giving advice and making suggestions about the resolution to a dispute because it implies that the parties would not otherwise accomplish that goal themselves.

Further threats to face that could occur in a mediation session might imply that one party has no concern for the other, which is a threat to their positive face or desire for social affirmation. For instance, when one party brings up irrelevant topics (wasting the time of others), interrupts, refuses to cooperate in the mediation, or inaccurately addresses the other person (using a first name if that is not preferred, or not using an appropriate title), that party exhibits little concern for the other. Certainly, as mediators, we would watch for interruptions and refusals to cooperate, because those things disrupt the communication environment we are trying to establish. However, we also need to consider that these actions could be face threatening to the other party as well. Just "correcting" that behavior may not be enough; rather, we may want to work on ways to reframe those actions before moving forward with the session.

Power is also an important part of understanding face and threats to face. Typically, the more power a person has in a relationship, the more acceptable we think it is for them to commit face threats. For example, we usually think it is acceptable for a teacher or a doctor to offer advice to a student or patient. However, it seems less appropriate for the student or patient to offer advice to the teacher or doctor. This is because the teacher and doctor are considered to have more power in these relationships. The same is true for other face threats, such as giving criticism or making requests. We generally think such actions are more acceptable from people in higher positions of power (parents, supervisors, community leaders, etc.).

However, the fact that we find these face threats more acceptable coming from people of power also becomes a major concern in mediation sessions, during which we try to *balance* power among the participants. We need to be careful that participants do not fall into communication patterns that keep them in an imbalanced power relationship. While it is important to recognize that relationships must continue *after* the mediation, it is also important that the participants feel like they have appropriate power to make a decision *during* a mediation session. If a teacher and a student are having a dispute about a grade, it is important to recognize that the teacher has a great deal of power in the relationship; however, the teacher should not take advantage of that power during the mediation session. Being careful to reframe and account for face threats from the teacher during that session will help the student feel more comfortable communicating about their interests and needs, and will help the dispute move toward resolution.

While face threats are important to recognize and understand in the mediation session, it is also important to understand that they cannot be entirely *prevented* from happening. Face threats occur every day in many different circumstances. In fact, we should not necessarily avoid making all threats to face; if we did so, we would probably avoid many conflicts that would otherwise be successfully resolved. The important concern for mediators is that we *account* for threats to face. If we have to offer criticism, we do so by softening the criticism. If we have to bring up uncomfortable topics (which could be seen as having little concern for the other person), we should do so by acknowledging that we know this is uncomfortable, but that it is also an important consideration to have (giving a reason). When we acknowledge that we know we are committing threats to face, but that we have good reasons for doing so, it helps the other person to better understand the situation and not take it as personally as they would without the accounting.

CASE 8.2
RACE, FACE AND POWER
———————————

A neighborhood mediation program received a call from a very upset principal of a middle school. He said that a Samoan mother had called the school several times blaming the principal for allowing racial prejudice in his school. She felt that the students, teachers, and staff picked on her daughter. He did not understand why the mother or daughter felt that way, so he called the mediation program to help.

The mediators asked the principal, the mother, and her thirteen-year-old daughter to attend the mediation. Because the principal had made the initial call to the mediators, they asked him to share his perspective and give some background. He explained that he did not understand the accusations made against him, and he denied any racial prejudice in the school. During the time that the principal was sharing his perspective, the girl's mother became quite agitated. She was very upset with the principal's denial, but the mediators explained that they would like the girl to share her perspective and asked the mother to wait to speak. However, when they asked the girl to talk about her perspectives, she refused and said she had nothing to say. The mediators suspected that she was too intimidated to share for some reason, so they asked her to meet with them outside of the mediation room in a caucus session.

Both the principal and the mother waited in separate rooms while the mediators met with the daughter in yet another room. The mediators asked the girl to share her perspective in confidence and she began to relate her experiences at the school. They listened to the daughter for about forty-five minutes as she talked about her experiences with what she interpreted as racial prejudice. She was intimidated about discussing this with her parents and the administration because she thought that they might make things even worse for her if she complained. At the end of the caucus session, she started to cry. When the mediators asked her why she was crying, she said that no one had ever taken the time to listen to her concerns about the way she was treated at school.

Even though they understood the girl's feelings of intimidation, the mediators asked if she would be willing, with their help, to share this information with the principal. She said that she was afraid of retaliation. She wanted to make sure that nothing she said would get back to other teachers or students at the school. When the mediators suggested that the girl could meet with them and the principal, but her mother could wait outside, she agreed. The mediators then asked the mother to wait in a separate room while they helped the daughter talk with the principal.

The girl asked the principal if something happened in the school or in a classroom that she felt was hurtful to her, if she could be sure that she not be singled out as the "complainer" when she talked to him about it. Since these things would affect other girls, she wanted to be sure that they all be called in to talk to him so that the teachers she was talking about would not think it was necessarily her who was complaining about their behavior. The principal agreed to this request and asked that, in return, the girl be honest with him about her experiences. He said that if they could be honest with each other, and be completely confidential about their discussions, that he would try to make the environment better. He also talked with the girl about what she would need to do to successfully graduate from her middle school.

When the principal and girl had signed the agreement, the mediators asked the mother to come back in the room. She demanded to see the agreement, but her daughter told her mother that the agreement was confidential and that it was between her and the principal. The mother was able to accept this when the mediators explained that they had worked with both the principal and the girl to make sure that they both felt comfortable with the agreement.

1. Why do you think the mother was so upset when the principal denied any racial prejudice at the school? Why did she want to talk to the mediators about it even though her daughter was the one involved?

    _____

    _____

    _____

2. Why was the daughter intimidated about talking about her experiences? Why do you think that it was important to the daughter that her mother not be in the room?

    _____

    _____

    _____

3. What were the power relationships in this mediation? How do you think the mediators worked to balance the power relationships?

    _____

    _____

    _____

CONCLUSION

Throughout this chapter, we have continued our discussion of sharing perspectives by introducing theories about interaction goals and face management. Understanding the strategic nature of communication and recognizing the strategies people use during a mediation session is helpful. This enables mediators to more insightfully interpret the communication of parties and help them to manage their communication more effectively and appropriately. Further, recognizing the importance of face, and accounting for threats to face, can help mediators understand the reactions that parties have to certain kinds of communicative acts. Knowing the kinds of acts to watch out for also helps prepare mediators in the appropriate use of the communication tools they have developed to both coach parties and model communication practices throughout the process.

CASE 8.3
THEME PARTIES

College campuses have witnessed an increasing number of parties with themes that are disturbing in their marketing and thematic components. These parties are touted as having good old "college fun." Some students feel these events continue to be held on campus even at the expense of offending certain individuals and groups. Still others believe that the themes seem to be more mean spirited than the sponsoring participants are letting on or intending. Themes that get the largest share of attention are those that seem to have social stigma and bias characteristics, such as: Ghetto Fabulous, White Trash, Pimps and Hoes, Gangsta, South of the Border, Cowboy and Indians, etc.

In one situation, a college student invited her African American roommate, and friend of one year, to come with her to a party. The African American student asked her roommate (who is not African American) what she should bring to the party and how she should dress. The friend said it was a "Ghetto Fabulous" party and she was dressing up in a short skirt, lots of makeup, big jewelry, and a cornrow-braided hairstyle. The African American roommate says she cannot go to a racist event that seeks to make fun of African American culture and community.

The African American student is shocked by her roommate's lack of sensitivity to a kind of bias that she sees as clear and problematic. The roommate is embarrassed and confused because she felt that she and her roommate had a very good understanding about ethnic issues. She is not a racist and would not do anything that she thought was biased. She thought going to the party was a way to show solidarity with her roommate and show her openness to African American culture. They had had many conversations about race relations, about hip-hop, and about being willing to become involved with each other's culture. She saw this party as a way to show their bond around cultural expression.

The African American roommate was dismayed that her roommate would consider going to a party with such a biased theme. She felt the roommate should know better, given the open conversations they had shared about historical cultural bias in American society. They had talked about general society's commodification of cultural attributes through the use of racial stereotypes, ethnic hazing comedy, and appropriation of music and hip-hop culture.

1. In this situation, it seems clear that even though the roommates had spent a lot of time with each other, and even talked about their differences, they still did not understand each other. Is it possible for them to ever understand each other if they are from different cultures?

    _____

    _____

    _____

2. How might the roommates' face and politeness concerns have affected their conversations until this point? How might they continue to affect them?

    _____

    _____

    _____

3. How could the two roommates have come to such different conclusions about the appropriateness of this theme party?

    _____

    _____

    _____

4. Is it possible for the roommates to understand each other's perspectives?

    _____

    _____

    _____

5. Will it ever be possible for these roommates to be as close as they were before this incident? (Hint: think about the things that might have made them good roommates to begin with).

    _____

    _____

    _____

9

Brainstorming
and Problem Solving

Sharing perspectives among the parties is, perhaps, the most difficult and important part of a mediation session. Since mediation focuses specifically on fostering understanding and healthy relationships, perspective sharing is essential to achieving the confidence and skills needed to enter into dispute resolution with clear interests and an understanding of the interdependent nature of conflict resolution. Once the parties have finished sharing perspectives, they are often ready to start actively working toward the goal with which many of them came into the mediation—to resolve their dispute. In this chapter, we discuss when and how to move parties from perspective sharing into problem solving. We also focus on the tools mediators can use to help them coach the parties toward this important and empowering end-goal of the mediation process.

MOVING FROM PERSPECTIVE SHARING TO BRAINSTORMING

Parties are ready to move on to brainstorming in a mediation session when they have exhausted the sharing of their perspectives. A mediator can successfully direct the move from perspective sharing to brainstorming by understanding two important signs to look for while parties are sharing their perspectives. During this process, it is important for mediators to remember that they are still communication process coaches. In other words, they make the decision of when to move the parties forward into this process, and they can always move the parties out of brainstorming and back into sharing perspectives if it seems that more discussion about interests and concerns is warranted.

One sign that the parties may be ready to move from perspective sharing into brainstorming is when the parties seem to be comfortably conversing with each other about their interests and needs, and when it seems clear that they are listening to and understanding each other. While a mediator may work with parties during this process to communicate effective active listening skills and to share and understand the perspective of the other parties, at some point the mediator may no longer feel the parties need a "coach." When the parties are interacting with each other by effectively using the skills in which the mediators have coached them, this is a sign that the parties are ready to move toward a successful brainstorming session.

Mediators should look for signs that the parties seem to be naturally moving toward brainstorming on their own. When parties begin to understand each other's perspectives, they will seem to move toward problem solving in their interactions. When mediators hear statements like "I didn't realize how important it was to you to remain anonymous in your complaints. I would be willing to make sure that happens in the future by making sure that everyone involved is a part of the conversation," it is a clear sign that the parties feel comfortable working interdependently toward a resolution to their problem.

When mediators see these signs, it becomes a turning point in the mediation. However, it is important to recognize these signs within the context of perspective sharing. Sometimes one party will be ready to move on, but another will not. Therefore, mediators need to make sure that all parties are ready and that all needs, interests, and concerns have been investigated before a move is made toward brainstorming. If one party seems to be hedging, it may be important to either return to perspective sharing or even hold a caucus to make sure that all parties are comfortable, and that the power in the relationships is effectively balanced for real resolution to occur.

When mediators believe that it is time to move from sharing perspectives to brainstorming, it is helpful to "check-in" with the parties to make sure that they are, indeed, ready. Make sure to ask them if they think that the other parties really understand their needs and concerns. As a mediator, if you believe that there is something that came up in the beginning of the mediation, but that seemed to be left behind, bring it up again. Ask the parties about that concern, and see if they would still like to work through it. You might ask something like "I remember that you were concerned about trash cans being left out during the day, but we haven't talked about that in a while. Do you think your concerns about the trash cans have been heard?" If there is something that one or more of the parties would still like to work through, stay in the sharing perspective stage a little longer and work through those things. Once the mediators have buy-in about moving forward, everyone can comfortably begin to work through the interests of all sides in a dispute.

BRAINSTORMING

When mediators feel like all of the parties' concerns and interests have been heard, and they have buy-in from the parties to move forward, it is time to move toward brainstorming. This can be an exciting time for everyone involved. Even though parties and mediators may be tired at this point, the excitement of being closer to a resolution can help to move everyone through the process. It is important for mediators to be clear about the ground rules of brainstorming, to take accurate and neutral notes during the brainstorming process, and to exhaust every possibility before moving on toward resolution.

Brainstorming is an effective communication process used in creative problem solving situations; it allows people to think of all possible solutions to a problem without fearing criticism for their ideas. Often used in organizations as a way to creatively work through problems and "think outside of the box," brainstorming is also quite effective in interpersonal problem solving such as mediations. Because the process is geared toward creative solutions, it is important to be clear about the ground rules of brainstorming. Here are a few that we like to use:

1. No idea is too crazy—if it comes into your head, state it.
2. Think about solutions at both the micro and macro levels—even if your solution idea only would solve a small aspect of the dispute, still mention it (it may be combined with other small ideas).
3. Build on other people's ideas. One person's idea may make you think of something similar, but a little different. Go ahead and mention it.
4. Take your time. Even though you may be excited to complete the process, creativity takes time—make sure to allow for that in the process.
5. Do not criticize ideas—even your own—at this point in the process. Every idea goes on the list—you can worry about criticizing ideas later when you are selecting possible solutions.
6. It's not quality, it's quantity! While we usually think of this in the reverse, during a brainstorming session, the more ideas the better, no matter how "good" they are.
7. The mediator should not participate in idea generation. It may be difficult to stay out of the mix, but no matter how good you think your idea might be, do not participate. Ideas need to come from the parties—the mediator only facilitates this process.

Following these ground rules allows for creativity and working together. The idea is that all parties in the dispute are working toward the same resolution—one that resolves all of the concerns for all of the parties, and one that focuses on all of the interests of all of the parties.

The first part of the brainstorming session should identify all of the interests and concerns the parties would like to work through. While the parties share perspectives with each other, they should also work toward identifying what interests they have in the dispute and what they need to leave with in order to feel that the dispute has been resolved. Ultimately, during perspective sharing, the parties begin to develop an understanding for the interests and needs of the other parties, in addition to making their own clear. In some cases, parties will have similar interests and needs. In other cases, parties will have different interests and needs. At the outset of the brainstorming session, it is important to create a list of all interests and needs of the parties so that ideas can be generated for all of them.

During the brainstorming session, the mediator will take notes on all of the ideas that are offered. It is important that no idea be omitted from the list to preserve the integrity of this communication practice. A number of models are available for mediators to use in note taking, and we have found that all of them work successfully, depending on how comfortable the mediator is with them. Thus, choose a method with which you feel comfortable and one that works with the resources that you have available.

Needs/Concerns

One method of note taking is for mediators to list all of the needs and concerns to be solved by the ultimate resolution. These should not be listed by party; in other words, do not create a sheet for Party A's needs and then another for Party B's needs. Simply list all of the needs and concerns spoken during the perspective sharing and do so in whatever order they occurred. Ask the parties if you have covered all of their needs and concerns to make sure that you have everything on the list. Then, as you take notes during the process, you can do so within "need" categories and ensure that the generated ideas cover all of the needs and concerns of the parties.

One way to execute this method is to use a white board or large notepaper on an easel. Listing the needs as different "columns" on the white board allows for the note-taking mediator to position the ideas under the need for which they are most relevant. If the resources are available, some mediators like to type the ideas into a table/spreadsheet on a computer and project the image onto a wall or screen. The mediator could create a separate column for each need in the table and then parties can keep track of the ideas by seeing them clearly organized on the screen.

Another method for note taking is for the mediator to write all of the ideas in whatever order they come up. As the brainstorming session progresses, a list of needs and concerns becomes available for everyone to look at and consider while brainstorming. Sometimes this method is more appropriate because many ideas might work toward resolving several needs all at once. Again, the mediator could do this using a white board or projected computer screen so that everyone can see the notes.

In some cases, you might find yourself in an environment without ideal resources for note taking. Maybe you are in a room without a whiteboard or easel, and maybe you do not have access to a computer or projector. If you are stuck with paper and pencil/pen notes, it is helpful to put yourself in a central location so that the parties can see what you are writing; it is also helpful to review ideas periodically during the brainstorming session. After five or six ideas are generated, you may review all of the ideas up to that point so that parties can continually think about and build upon those ideas.

No matter what method of note taking you use, it is important to create *neutral* lists. Refrain from taking notes on which you make clear which party came up with which idea. Your notes should always reflect a neutral stance. Because brainstorming and problem solving should be interdependent activities, it does not matter who came up with the ideas in the long run. What matters is whether all of the parties agree to the final resolution. However, if you find that one party is dominating the brainstorming process, use your power balancing skills to help the quieter party to generate as many ideas as possible. In many cases, one party might suggest a solution, but both parties have been considering it. We often hear, "I was thinking the same thing!" during brainstorming sessions.

Concluding the Brainstorming Session

While it is important not to conclude a brainstorming session prematurely, the time comes when mediators and parties believe that they have reached an exhaustive list of ideas. At this point, we often ask the parties to take a minute or two to peruse the list of ideas and see if they would like to add something else to the list. When there is nothing more to add, it is important to ask the parties if they are ready to move toward resolution of their dispute. Once they agree, the mediators can shift from brainstorming into problem solving.

There are a few important questions to ask at this point of the brainstorming session:

1. Have the parties generated some ideas for every need or concern outlined at the beginning of the brainstorming session?
2. Are there other needs or concerns that might have come up during the brainstorming process that were not on the initial list? If so, have the parties considered ideas for those needs and concerns as well?

3. Would the parties like to have more time? In some cases, parties may want to take a break from the process and come back to it to make sure that they have considered everything. Sometimes, just taking a break to use the restroom or get a cup of tea helps parties to refresh and think of things they initially missed.

If everyone is confident that they would like to move forward, then the mediators can move toward the first step in resolution.

PROBLEM SOLVING

When mediators start problem solving during the mediation process, they will focus on the list created during the brainstorming process as well as the list of needs and concerns the parties generated for brainstorming. Again, as in brainstorming, the mediator only facilitates this process. While you may be tempted, take care to refrain from offering your own criticism or suggestions as you take the parties through this process.

There are two ways the mediator might approach the problem solving session. First, the mediator will ask the parties which ideas they like the most and either circle them or write them on a different list. The mediator will take care to make sure that all parties agree on the selected ideas. After the ideas are selected from the overall list of brainstormed ideas, the mediator will ask parties if this list of ideas covers all of the interests and needs that were identified. If it does not, then the parties should be encouraged to work through some of the other ideas to ensure that all of their interests and needs are represented. If the new list covers all interests and needs, the mediator will help the parties work through a reality check.

A second way the mediator might approach problem solving is to start with the list of interests and needs and go down the list to find which idea the parties agree is the best one to address each interest and need. In some cases, the same idea may be listed under a few different categories; in others, there will be different ideas listed for each interest and need. In this scenario, the mediator would systematically go through each interest and need, and work through an acceptable idea to resolve each before going on to the next one.

As parties discuss each of the ideas that they like, make sure to practice the same kind of communication that took place during perspective sharing. Specifically, make sure that all parties are able to address any concerns they have about the ideas, and make sure that you continue to balance the power and communication among the parties. Parties will need to have every opportunity to work through their concerns surrounding each idea before they buy into the resolution.

REALITY CHECKING

Whichever method the mediator uses to go through the list of brainstormed ideas, once an idea has been agreed upon that meets every interest and need, the mediator needs to facilitate the parties in a reality-checking exercise. For every idea that the parties agreed upon, the mediator will ask them the following questions:

1. What could prevent this idea from working? Even if we agree to this idea now, what could happen in the future to prevent this idea from working out?

2. What happens if everyone agrees to the ideas, but for whatever reason, one of the parties does not follow through? What would you like to do in that scenario?

In asking these questions, the mediator pushes the issue about whether these ideas are workable solutions. In some cases, parties are in such a collaborative mood after the perspective sharing that they might have the best intentions of following through with an idea, but find that in practice, the idea is a little more difficult to work with than they had originally thought. Mediators need to anticipate this possibility and ask the parties to work through these potentially problematic scenarios. If the answer to the first question leads parties to believe that an idea may not be as workable as they originally thought, they will need to try to work through another idea that makes more sense and is more workable than the first.

Answers generated to the second question are more global. What if, after signing the agreement, something happens causing one or more of the parties to noncompliance with the agreement? While this is not a common occurrence, it does happen. Thus, the parties should come up with some contingency clause. If the agreement does not work, will they come back to the mediation table? Will they try to work it out themselves in some fashion? What procedure would they use? Pushing parties to consider these contingencies helps to make sure that the agreement is complete, but it also helps them anticipate how they will work to resolve their differences in the future. Ideally, they will have learned about themselves and the other parties while sharing perspectives and will have some ideas about how they can work through these issues on their own in the future.

ASSURING BUY-IN AND WRITING THE AGREEMENT

After completing the reality check, and the mediators and parties are confident that they have reached an agreement, the mediators should write out the agreement for the parties. Depending on resources, this may be done on a word processor or by hand. The mediators need to take special care that all aspects of the agreement are written in appropriate detail, and they should make sure that the parties agree that all of the necessary detail is included in the agreement. When all parties have read the agreement and have assured the mediators that they agree with it, they will then sign the document, along with the mediators, and all appropriate parties should be given a copy. Consider the following sample of a mediation agreement.

Figure 9.1: Example Mediation Agreement Form

MEDIATION AGREEMENT

In the matter of mediation between:

Participant 1_____

Participant 2_____

We, the undersigned, having participated in a mediation session on ___/___/___ and being satisfied that the provisions of the resolution of our dispute are fair and reasonable, hereby agree to abide by and fulfill the following:

> *List all of the agreed upon ideas here, including any contingency plans agreed upon if the parties do not follow through.*
>
> *If the parties decide that others outside of the mediation may also see this document, make sure to list those people in this box as well so that it is clear that everyone agrees.*

Participant 1_____

Participant 2_____

Witnessed: We, the undersigned mediators being in accordance with the mediation agreement entered into by the above signed and dated ___/___/___, and having heard these Participants resolve their dispute, hereby affirm and witness the above agreement.

Mediator 1_____

Mediator 2_____

FOLLOWING THROUGH WITH PARTIES

While the resolution to an agreement may seem like the end of the mediation process, it is not. The mediators and the parties have worked diligently to create a resolution to their dispute; because the parties have created the resolution themselves, it will most likely be successful. However, after some time has passed, it is important to follow up with the parties to make sure that the agreement is working for them and to see if they have other concerns or questions with which mediators may be of assistance.

Mediators and parties need to work through the process in good faith; that is, they need sincerely and honestly to work toward appropriate and effective management of the disputes that come to the table. Part of having good faith for the mediators is that they consider that the parties may need some help maintaining their agreement or remembering the conviction with which they decided on the agreement during the mediation session. We typically suggest that mediators or case developers contact participants somewhere between four and eight weeks after a mediation to check in with them and make sure the agreement is working out. During this check-in process, the mediators should find out the following:

1. Are parties still following the agreement? Is the agreement working for them, or have they worked out something else in the meantime? The purpose of this is to let the parties know that the mediators support them and would like to help them if there are any problems.

2. Did the mediation process work for the parties? Do the parties think the process was worthwhile? Was there something they would have changed or done differently? The purpose of this is to learn more about how the mediators can improve the process for future mediation sessions.

While finding out the answers to the above questions, in some cases it will be important for mediators to keep records concerning their experiences with disputing parties. While agreements are held in confidence, mediators sometimes keep records about how many of their mediations ended in a resolution, how many of them did not end in resolution but were eventually resolved, and how many of the disputes were unable to resolve their problems through mediation or on their own. Depending upon what organization you work with as a mediator, whether for a community or corporate organization, or on your own, keeping a record of the results of your mediation sessions may help to disseminate the value of the mediation process.

When Mediations "Do Not Work"

While this is a difficult concept to grasp at first, we believe that mediations are *always* successful. Whether an agreement is reached or not, the process of mediation brings parties together in a way that helps them attempt to understand each other. Sometimes, this does not happen the way that we hoped it would. There are times when parties may leave a mediation session disappointed that they were unable to resolve their dispute, and the mediators may feel (unjustifiably in our opinion) that they have failed in helping the parties come to a resolution. However, no matter what the outcome of a mediation, the following will have occurred:

1. The parties have been exposed to a process of conflict management that encourages them to view the perspective of other parties and to focus on their interests rather than their positions.

2. The parties will have learned about themselves during this process because the mediators will have coached them through communication practices that they may not have used before.

3. The parties will understand that there are people in the world who care about and will listen to their perspectives.

People who participate in mediation often tell us that they thought it was a valuable experience; they realized that, even if they could not resolve the dispute, they may be able to work through other disputes more effectively and appropriately. When no agreement is reached, the mediators should remind themselves and the parties that communicating with each other and attempting to understand each other is always a valuable exercise.

Works Cited

Barkai, J. (1992). Applying the Hawaiian mediation model to disputes and conflicts, *Interspectives, 11*, 40.

Brown, P. & Levinson, S. (1987). *Politeness: Some universals in language use.* Cambridge: Cambridge University Press.

Canary, D. J., Spitzberg, B. H. & Semic, B. A. (1998). The experience and expression of anger in interpersonal settings. In P.A. Andersen, L. K. Guerrero (Eds.) *Handbook of Communication and Emotion: Research, Theory, Applications and Context*, San Diego: Academic Press, pp. 189–213.

Carpenter, S. & Halberstadt, A. G. (1996). What makes people angry? Laypersons' and psychologists' categorizations of anger in family relationships. *Cognition and Emotion, 10*, 627–656.

DaSilva, A. (2006, February 2). Judge urges Hawaiian mediation rite. Associated Press. Retrieved:
http://boston.com/news/nation/articles/2006/02/02judge_urges_hawaiian_mediation_rite/

Dillard, J. P., Segrin, C. & Harden, J. H. (1989). Primary and secondary goals in the production of interpersonal influence messages. *Communication Monographs, 56*, 19–38.

Dugan, M. & Dunne, T. (2002). The Lizard Brain. *Articles and Musings*, available:
http://www.instantbrainstorm.com/lizard_brain.html.

Dweck, C. S. (2000). *Self-theories: Their role in motivation, personality and development.* Lillington, NC: Edward Brothers.

Goldberg, S., Sander, F. & Rogers, N. (1999). *Dispute Resolution.* Boston, MA: Little, Brown & Co.

Fisher, R., Ury W. L. & Patton, B. (1992). *Getting to yes: Negotiating agreement without giving in.* New York: Penguin Books.

Goffman, E. (1967). *Interaction Ritual.* New York: Pantheon Books.

Gottman, J. (2001). Meta-emotion, children's emotional intelligence and buffering children from marital conflict. In C. D. Ryff, B. H. Singer (Eds.) *Emotion, Social Relationships and Health*, New York: Oxford University Press, pp. 23–40.

Guerrero, L. K. & La Valley, A. G. (2006). Conflict, emotion and communication. In J. G. Oetzel and S. Ting-Toomey (Eds.), *The Sage Handbook of Conflict Communication*, Thousand Oaks, CA: Sage, 69–96.

Kanahele, G. H. S. (1986). *Ku Kanaka Stand Tall: A Search for Hawaiian Values.* Honolulu: University of Hawaii Press.

Lazarus R. S. (1991). Cognition and motivation in emotion. *American Psychologist, 46*(4), 352–367.

Lefcourt, H. M. (1976). Locus of control and the response to aversive events. *Canadian Psychological Review, 17*(3), 202–209.

MacGeorge, E. L. (2001). Support providers' interaction goals: The influence of attributions and emotions. *Communication Monographs, 68*, 72–97.

Parise, C. M. (2004). *Assertiveness training: A training and development project for Downtown College Preparatory High School.* Unpublished master's project, San Jose State University, San Jose, CA.

Petronio, S. (2000). The boundaries of privacy: Praxis of everyday life. In S. Petronio (Ed.), *The Secrets of Private Disclosures.* Mahwah, NJ: Erlbaum.

Rotter, J. (1954). *Social learning and clinical psychology.* Englewood Cliffs, NJ: Prentice Hall.

Sabee, C. M. (2007). *Secondary goals in boundary management: Choosing to bring in a third party (or not).* Unpublished manuscript.

Sabee, C.M., Bylund, C. L., Imes, R.S., Sanford, A. A. & Rice, I.S. (2007). Patients' attributions for health-care provider responses to patients' presentation of internet health research. *Southern Communication Journal, 72*(3), 265–284.

Sabee, C. M. & Wilson, S. R. (2005). Students' primary goals, attributions and facework during conversations about disappointing grades. *Communication Education 54*(3), 185–204.

Scherer, K. R. & Wallbott, H. G. (1994). Evidence for universality and variation of differential emotion response patterning. *Journal of Personality and Social Psychology, 66*, 310–328.

Shaver, P., Schwartz, J. & Kirson, D. (1987). Emotion knowledge: Further exploration of a prototype approach. *Journal of Personality and Social Psychology, 52*, 1061–1086.

Shook, V. (1986). *Ho'oponopono: Contemporary uses of a Hawaiian problem solving process.* Honolulu: University of Hawaii Press.

Trenholm, S. & Jensen, A. (2008). *Interpersonal Communication, 6th Ed.* New York: Oxford University Press.

Vace, N. A, DeVaney, S. B. & Wittmer, J. (1995). *Experiencing and Counseling Multicultural and Diverse Populations, 3rd Ed.,* Levittown, PA: Taylor and Francis.

Vangelisti, A. L. (1994). Couples' communication problems: The counselor's perspective. *Journal of Applied Communication Research, 22*(2), 106–126.

Wall, J. A. & Callister, R. R. (1995). Ho'oponopono: Some lessons from Hawaiian mediation. *Negotiation Journal, 11*(1), 45–54.

Weiner, B. (1986). *An attributional theory of motivation and emotion.* New York: Springer Verlag.

Wilson, S. R., Aleman, C. G. & Leatham, G. B. (1998). Identity implications of influence goals: A revised analysis of face-threatening acts and application to seeking compliance with same sex friends. *Human Communication Research, 25*, 64–96.

Wilson, S. R., & Sabee, C. M. (2003). Explicating communicative competence as a theoretical term. In J. O. Greene & B. R. Burleson (Eds.), *Handbook of communication and social interaction skills* (pp. 3–50). Hillsdale, NJ: Lawrence Erlbaum.

Appendix A
Tips on Successful Role-Playing

Throughout this course, as you practice working through mediation skills, you will be using a process called role-playing. You and two or three other people will play the parts of mediator and parties so that you can practice the communication coaching and modeling that is central to the process of mediation.

When you are playing the part of a mediator, you should be playing yourself. This will give you a chance to practice communication skills and different models so that you can decide for yourself what works for you. It also gives you some experience with the process of mediation before you mediate an actual dispute.

You will also be expected to play the parts of different parties in a dispute. This is for two reasons: First, it gives the colleagues in your class or training group the opportunity to practice mediation skills for themselves. Second, it gives you a chance to explore the perspectives of people other than yourself in a dispute. When you play the role of a party in a dispute, it is important that you understand that role as much as you can before the mediation begins. You will consider how the party would act, what the party would say, and what the party would feel. As you perform the experiences of this person, you should do so with a sincere understanding of the person's perspective.

You should ask yourself the following questions regarding the disputing party:

1. What assumptions does this person make about the dispute? What attributions have been made? What goals has the person set?

2. What is this person's cultural or social background, and how might that influence communication and participation in the mediation?

3. What are this person's interests and needs? What is the person feeling in this dispute?

4. What does this person need the other party(ies) to hear and understand about him before they go forward?

As you play the role of the party, try to act as sincerely and realistically as possible. It is not your role to "challenge" your colleagues who are playing the mediators; rather, your role is to give them as *real* an experience as possible. That said, it is also not your role to make it *easy* for them.

Finally, it is important to recognize that disputing parties often have strong emotions during a dispute. If you are really "into" the role, you may start to feel some of these emotions. Try to remember that you are playing a person other than yourself during this role. Sometimes it is helpful to give yourself a different name while playing a role so that when you are in character your name is different from when you are out of character.

Appendix B
Role-Play Practice Suggestions

As you work through role-plays in this class, you might want to try a few different "twists" to help you work on specific skill sets. Your instructor may suggest using certain of these twists in specific situations when you are practicing a particular skill set. However, at other times, you may find that you would like to practice a skill set more thoroughly during one of your role-plays. Feel free to use the following ideas to help with that.

1. *Identifying Reframing Statements:* For some assistance in recognizing which statements in a dispute should be reframed, give each of the parties a "flag" that they can use during the mediation session (we have used red squares of paper). During the dispute, when one party feels that another party said something that upset them or that they feel should be reframed, they should throw in a "flag" to let you know that you should reframe that statement. If you are having difficulty understanding why one of the parties threw a flag, then pause the mediation role play for a moment to discuss the statement.

2. *What do I do next?* Sometimes beginning mediators cannot decide what they should do next. You may find yourself feeling like this in your first few role-plays. Before the mediation starts, put together a list of questions that you could ask that concern the *process* of mediation. Then, give your parties "hints" that they can give you during the mediation that can help you decide what to do next. For instance, you may give your parties direction to hold up two fingers if you need to address concerns that have not been aired yet. Or, you might ask them to tap their pencils if they think they need a caucus. This exercise not only helps you think about all of the different options you have as a mediator (by putting together the list of process questions and "hints"), but also it helps you recognize when these things should happen in the process by trusting the instincts of your "parties."

Appendix C
Role-Plays

As you work through these role-plays, decide before you read them who is to play which part. Then, as you prepare for the role-plays, please read ONLY the part assigned to you. Because each of the parties will be playing their roles to the best of their ability, it is important to give them some latitude in interpreting that role. Thus, if you read the role ahead of time, you may come into the mediation with assumptions about it that your party does not necessarily have.

If you are playing the role of one of the parties, make sure to play the role as sincerely as you can. You can take some liberties with the roles to make them more realistic, but make sure that you follow the basic structure of your assigned role, so that the dispute has some truth to it as well.

ROLE-PLAY I
TRASH TALK

This role-play has three characters: The mediator (*there could be two mediators*), Lisa and Tom are the disputing parties. Please pick one of these roles to prepare for your role-play.

Mediator: You have been asked to mediate a dispute between two neighbors, Lisa and Tom, who have been having a disagreement about the location of trash cans in their yards. Lisa, the neighbor who called mediation services, is upset that Tom's trash cans end up in her yard on trash day. Tom does not believe it is his fault.

Lisa: You called mediation services because you have been having a problem with your neighbor, Tom. Every week on Monday night, Tom puts out the trash on the left side of his driveway, which borders your yard. Every Tuesday, you find that trash and recycling from their trash cans littered all over your yard. You know that it is because there are some homeless people who come by and go through the trash cans at night looking for recycling, and that is why you put your trash out early on Tuesday morning instead of on Monday night. Since you have to get up to commute to work each day at about 5:00 a.m., it is not a problem for you to do that. And it is really important for you to have a nice looking yard—so you end up having to pick up trash (which you find a little demeaning) every Tuesday night when you get home from work. You are getting frustrated with picking up all of this trash in your yard, which is not even your trash! You have tried calling Tom on Monday night when you see his trash is out to ask him to wait, but no one answers the phone—even though you know someone is home. That really gets to you—it is completely rude for your neighbors to ignore you like that. Also, you have tried to walk over and talk to your neighbor during the day, but no one seems to be home.

Tom: Mediation services called you to come in and mediate with your neighbor, Lisa. Frankly, if it will keep Lisa from bothering you all the time in the future, you are willing to be there. You have also been upset with her. Lisa's been bugging you about trash that gets in her yard on trash day—but trash gets in **everyone's** yard on trash day! It's like she thinks that you are throwing the trash over there, which you obviously would not do. Also, Lisa has this habit of trying to call you in the evening right about the time that your baby falls asleep. You have a new-born baby who you are trying to get to sleep through the night and whenever someone calls in the evening, it inevitably wakes her up. For the past few weeks, you periodically get calls from Lisa (you have caller id) at exactly the time that your baby is almost asleep.Like clockwork, your baby wakes up to the phone ringing, and you have to spend the next hour trying to get her back to sleep. It is rude for someone to be calling a family with a newborn at 8:00 p.m. at night anyway, and Lisa never even leaves a message.

ROLE-PLAY 2
PRICELESS PIECES

(Written by C. Hernandez-Robbins, SJSU, 2006)

This role-play has three characters: The mediator (*there could be two mediators*), Terry and Chris are the disputing parties.

Mediator: Terry and Chris are neighbors in the residence hall, and they have gotten into conflicts recently over noise and borrowed items. Last week the Resident Assistant on the floor overheard a shouting match between them. Later, Chris approached the RA and complained about a broken pottery piece, insisting that Terry pay for it. The RA recommended that they take their case to the campus mediation center.

Terry: You're really tired of the hassles caused by your neighbor in the dorms, Chris. Chris is a big partier, and several nights a week he and his friends play loud music and talk and laugh until late—midnight or even 1:00 a.m. On several occasions, you have gone over and knocked on his door asking him to keep the noise down. Fifteen minutes later, the volume is blaring again. You have an early morning paper route to pay your college bills and need to be asleep by 10:00 p.m. Sunday through Thursday nights.

Chris also borrows your things/belongings. No problem with borrowing—that's okay with you, but he doesn't return things to your room (your tennis racket, for example, one of dozens of examples) unless you go after them. When you get items back, they are dirty (e.g., popcorn popper).

Last week you were finishing a major paper. You needed a book that you had checked out of the library and you couldn't find it anywhere. After searching your entire room, you suddenly had an idea and checked Chris' room. Sure enough, there it stood on his bookshelf. Irritated, you yanked it down. Another book fell from the shelf and landed on a little pottery trinket below the desk. You were in a hurry and quite mad at Chris, so you left the broken pieces there.

An hour later, Chris banged on your door. When you opened it, he began swearing at you. When he refused to let you explain, you slammed the door in his face after telling him to come back and talk after he had cooled down.

Chris: Your neighbor in the dorm, Terry, has been a real pain lately. He is always hassling you about your stuff. Nothing is good enough for him. For example, he is always complaining about the noise when you have some of your friends over in the evening, even though no one else on the floor seems to mind. You are not trying to give him a hard time, but you get tired of being bugged, especially the way Terry handles it; he acts as though you are inferior.

Last week, you needed a library book. The librarian said it was checked out to Terry.

He wasn't around, but Phil, his roommate found it for you on Terry's desk. After you reminded Phil that Terry has often let you borrow his things, Phil said you could borrow the book for a few hours. You put the book on your bookshelf and went to supper. When you returned one and a half hours later, the book was gone and a clay sculpture you purchased in Mexico several years ago lay broken on your desk. You knew right away who had done it.

Upset, you went over and knocked on Terry's door. But when he saw who it was, he just told you to "cool it" and slammed the door in your face. Since then, you haven't spoken.

ROLE-PLAY 3
REPEATED REVIVALS

This role-play has three characters: the Mediator (*there could be two of you*), Dan and Robert are the two disputing parties.

Mediator: You were contacted to mediate a dispute between Dan and Robert. From what you understand, Dan called mediation services because he feels that he and Robert cannot come to an agreement on their own about how to deal with some noise complaints. Apparently, Dan has complained repeatedly of excessive noise coming from Robert's house, which is right next door. Rather than go to court, Dan contacted the free mediation service offered by their community.

Dan: You have been living in your house for about four years and you really enjoy your neighborhood for the most part. Robert moved in about one and a half years ago and things seemed fine, except that you never really saw him. While you thought it was odd that your neighbor was not friendly or around very much, you believe that you need to respect people's privacy and so you let him be. However, about four months ago, you started to have trouble sleeping at night because there were loud noises coming from Robert's house. Sometimes it sounds like loud music or fighting, and it keeps you up past midnight—at times. even past 1:00 a.m. Since you work an early shift that starts at 7:00 a.m., staying up that late has made you sleep deprived. You tried to call Robert, but you got no response. You tried to wait outside for him on the weekends but you never see him. You are extremely frustrated and you just need to get some sleep.

Robert: You moved to the area about eighteen months ago because you needed to get away from your environment. Previously, you had been living in an urban mid-western city, but your friends and family there did not seem to understand you, and you wanted to make a new start. Specifically, you were really searching for some spiritual guidance, and the traditions with which you grew up were not giving you what you needed. You had heard about a group in this area that you were interested in joining and so you moved here, got a new job, and have been basically happy. The group that you have found is very supportive and you find yourself happier than you've ever been. Three times a week, your group holds revivals at a member's house and you find them extremely uplifting. You also are involved in many community service projects because of the group and feel great about that. However, you find yourself in mediation today because your neighbor has been complaining about the revival meetings at your house. You have not felt comfortable talking to your neighbor because every time you talk about your group to someone outside of it, they laugh or tell you it is a cult or something. Moreover, it is not really that loud and it only happens at your house once a week or so. Evenings are the only time that your group can get together and you feel responsible to hold the event at your house at least once a week because you are an active member, and you care about the group.

ROLE-PLAY 4
STARVING STUDENTS

This role-play has three characters: the Mediator (*there could be two of you*), Kevin and David are the disputing parties.

Mediator: You have been asked to mediate a dispute between a university sophomore and his father. This student called mediation services with the complaint that his father was going to stop paying for his education and is making the student live at home. The student wants to continue with school; he does not want to live at home, but neither does he want to alienate his family in the process.

Kevin: You have been attending San Jose State University for a year and a half and have been living on campus during that time. You are originally from Fremont, which is not too far away; however, living on campus has been important for you as a step in gaining your independence. When you started school, you made a deal with your family that you would pay for your own housing (in the dorms) and they would pay for your school with money they had set aside in a special education account for you. You love school and are really excited about your major in Justice Studies. However, you received some bad news over the winter break. Your father told you that your brother (a sophomore in high school) has been having a tough time at school and he is worried that your brother may be getting into "the wrong crowd." Your father confided to you that your brother has almost been arrested twice, but has gotten out of it because your father vouched for him. Your father wants you to leave school, and come and live at home so that your family can be together during this troubling time. You really do not want to leave school, and you do not understand why this is your responsibility (after all, your brother is his own person!). You called mediation services to help you talk to your father about this.

David: Your child has been attending college for almost two years now and you are really proud of him. Up until now, you have had an agreement with your child that you would pay for school and your child would pay for his housing since he wanted to live on campus. Even though you live close to SJSU (in Fremont) you believed that having your child live on campus was a good idea to help him establish his independence. However, in the past year, your youngest son has been having serious troubles with school. You think he might be involved with drugs and he was almost arrested two times. Once, he was trying to use a fake ID to buy beer and the other time he was shoplifting cigarettes. His grades have also dropped dramatically and you are afraid that your son will not be able to attend college because he is really messing up. Your family has always been close, and you think it is important to stick up for one another. You have asked your older child to leave school and come home in order to help out the younger son. You really believe that having the family together right now could help your younger son through this tough time, and that it might make the difference between your son living a good life or not. You know that your older son really wants to continue with school, but you believe that the family needs to pull together in a crisis like this one.

ROLE-PLAY 5
SMOKING SECESSION

This role-play has three characters: the Mediator (*there could be two of you*), Karen and Susan are the two disputing parties.

Mediator: You were contacted to mediate a dispute between Karen and Susan. From what you understand, Karen called mediation services because she feels that she and Susan cannot come to an agreement on their own about how to divide the workload for a major project they are completing. Both parties work in the same office and have been working together for two years. Their supervisor recommended that they attend mediation because if he had to settle the dispute, he would have to write them up in their permanent personnel files.

Karen: You have been working in the same office with Susan for two years, and things had been going fine until about four months ago. Typically, you do not have to work closely with anyone else at the office, but your company has recently asked you to work with Susan to prepare a major advertising campaign for their community outreach program. Specifically, you have been working on a campaign to stop teens from smoking. This is an important cause for you, and you have been working extremely hard on it. Your younger brother was diagnosed with lung cancer, which was caused by smoking, and it is important for you to prevent this from happening to others. Further, you are up for a promotion in another three months, and you would like to have finished this major project and done it well as evidence of your abilities. The problem is that Susan has not been pulling her weight! You feel like you have been doing the bulk of the work; Susan has not been reliable or available for meetings and discussion. Unfortunately, you have other work to do as well, and you would like to spend more time with your family. You really need Susan to step up and do her share of the work on this project.

Susan: You have been working in the same office with Karen for two years. You believe that things have been going pretty well—usually you see each other, are cordial to each other, and do not have to work together that much. Recently, however, your company asked you to work with Karen on this community outreach campaign to stop teens from smoking. While you agreed to participate, you also are not that excited about it because it is just one more project on your plate—and your plate is already full! Moreover, it is just a community outreach campaign—it does not make your company any money at all (it just makes them look good to the community), and you think that your time is better spent working on increasing profit for your company. In addition, you and your spouse had a child about one year ago and it is important for you to not work really long hours—45 hours is enough as far as you are concerned. The problem is that Karen has been nagging you constantly about working on this project and it is getting out of hand. You simply do not have time to deal with this project, or with her nagging you about it.